Life in the

Gray

Finding Grace in the Blurry

Krista T. Kenney PhD

Contents

Preface

♥

G race is often misunderstood. Some see it as mere kindness, a
passive quality reserved for the gentle-hearted. Others confuse it with tolerance, assuming that to extend grace means to ignore
wrongdoing. But grace is neither passive nor blind. It is a force like an
act of defiant love in the face of imperfection. It exists in the gray areas
of life: between right and wrong, between pain and healing, between
expectation and reality. It is not about perfection or control but about
surrendering to what is while still choosing how to respond.

The invitation to grace is extended to all of us, but it requires a heart
posture of humility and compassion. Through the pages of this book,
I will explore how grace has shaped my life through personal failures,
deep disappointments, and even moments of extraordinary joy. You
will be challenged to reflect on your own journey and, hopefully, begin
to see grace as the thread that weaves through every human experience.

But what does it mean to accept this invitation? It requires a willingness to embrace the messiness of life. It calls us to relinquish control, to let go of the need for certainty, and to step into the unknown
with trust. Grace is found not in rigid rules, but in the fluid, un-
predictable rhythms of life. It is discovered in the moments when we

choose love over judgment, compassion over criticism, and faith over fear.

In this book, we will take a journey through the many facets of grace. We will examine how grace meets us in our brokenness, in our relationships, and in the uncertainties of life. We will explore the power of self-grace and the necessity of extending grace to others. And ultimately, we will discover how grace is not merely something we receive, but it is something we live.

So, take a breath. Open your heart. And step into the invitation to grace.

Foreword

♥

Grace is a concept we often talk about but rarely take the time to truly understand. It is not just a theological idea; it is a way of life, a mindset, and a gift freely given. This book is not just my story. It is a reflection of the grace that we all experience in different ways. My hope is that as you read these pages, you will see grace not as an abstract principle, but as something tangible and transformative.

Whether you are in a season of brokenness, transition, waiting, or healing, my prayer is that this book helps you embrace grace as a daily practice. Thank you for allowing me to share this journey with you. May these words encourage, inspire, and lead you to a deeper understanding of the grace that holds us all.

Introduction

♥

Grace is the power to show up in my brokenness and be seen through my own filth. It is the empowerment to transform into something and someone greater. Grace is the depth of love I receive when I least deserve it. It is given in moments of mercy when I find myself at my lowest. It comes when my faith wavers, when my anxiety takes hold, and when I struggle to make sense of life's mysteries.

Grace is not an abstract theological concept. Instead it is deeply personal. I have found grace in the darkest seasons of my life: through my parents' painful divorce, the battle with poverty, the devastation of pregnancy loss, and the daily struggles of parenthood. In these moments, grace was not a distant idea; it was the sustaining force that carried me through.

But what does grace look like in everyday life? It is the gentle encouragement of a friend who refuses to let you drown in self-doubt. It is the unexpected kindness of a stranger who pays for your coffee on a day when you feel invisible. It is the still, small voice within that whispers, "You are enough," when the weight of inadequacy presses down on your shoulders. Grace is woven into the ordinary moments of life, transforming them into sacred encounters.

Grace is:

- Holding space for uncertainty.

- Moving through pain with self-compassion.

- Releasing the weight of resentment.

- Allowing yourself to be human.

Through personal stories, biblical insights, and reflections, this book will take you on a journey to discovering grace in the places you least expect it.

Chapter One

♥

"My grace is sufficient for you, for power is made perfect in weakness."

2 Corinthians 12:9 (NRSV)

In our deepest moments of brokenness, God doesn't demand strength. He offers grace. Not after the healing, not once we've figured it out, but right there in the middle of the mess.

Chapter Summary

This chapter explores the kind of brokenness that doesn't just come from personal failure or loss, but from the slow unraveling of a life you once knew. As a child, I watched my family split apart. What followed wasn't just divorce. It was a painful season of emotional and financial instability, displacement, and grief that lingered long after the shouting stopped.

The emotional tension of this chapter is rooted in the confusion and silence that often follows childhood trauma. How do you hold space for parents who hurt you, but also tried their best? How do you carry the weight of abandonment, shame, and loss while still believing in love, in healing, in God?

This is where grace begins to work. Grace met me not with answers, but with presence. Through small moments of compassion, unexpected support, and the long process of perspective and healing, I came to see that grace doesn't eliminate brokenness. It transforms how we carry it.

Where Grace Met Me: Grace in the Unraveling

I don't look like what I've been through. I'd say the same for my closest relationships in that we are all walking miracles of survival, stitched together by grace. It is only by God's mercy that I've been able to forgive myself and others, to keep showing up, to keep trying again after failure or offense.

My earliest lesson in grace came through heartbreak. One spring afternoon, my parents picked me up from school. I was just a child, tucked into the back seat, unaware that my world was about to fall apart. What began as bickering between my parents quickly escalated. My father jumped out of the moving vehicle and walked home. Moments later, I watched him throw his clothes into bags and leave our home for good.

Nothing was ever the same.

That moment marked the unraveling of my childhood. My older brother left for college, and my mother moved my sister and me from

North Carolina to Georgia. We didn't land anywhere for long. We moved town to town, house to house, a new school nearly every year. Then came her pregnancy with a boyfriend who entered and exited like a storm, leaving behind emotional wreckage and confusion. The one bright light from that chaos was the birth of my baby brother. His tiny presence reminded me that even in the darkest season, God births beauty. I was learning, even then, that we live in the gray where joy and pain coexist.

It would take years for me to name that season as one of *grace*.

The financial strain was constant. At one point, the school bus picked me up from a hotel where we were living. I remember the shame. I remember the silence I kept. My sister soon left for college, and I found myself in a quiet house with only my mom and baby brother. My father, now far away, still pastored one of the largest churches and held a respected position in the community. The contrast was dizzying with poverty and prestige existing on opposite ends of my own family tree.

I felt invisible. I kept my struggles hidden, focused on excelling at school, and convinced myself no one could understand the heaviness I carried. But God did. And in the loneliness, He sent me an angel in the form of a girl named Stacy who saw me, who didn't judge me. Through her, I found my way to a Christian student group. Friends' parents began picking me up for Bible study and youth events. Although both of my parents were pastors, it wasn't until then that I began building *my* relationship with God.

That season didn't immediately become easier, but it became sacred.

I came to see my parents differently. As people. As humans carrying their own pain. My mom, despite our lack, used her social capital to barter services so I could attend a private school. My dad, despite his responsibilities, drove hours to see me perform, picking me up for weekends when he could. They didn't always get it right, but they showed up.

As I grew older, I saw them offer grace to each other too. I watched them co-parent with kindness. They put their wounds aside to ensure that I, their daughter, could still have a whole family in some form. Because of that grace, I celebrated holidays with both parents in the same room. Today, my children go on vacations with both grandparents present. What a gift. What a testimony.

Divorce is messy. It's a gray space where love and pain collide. But even there, grace exists. It's in the willingness to show up when showing up is hard. It's in the decision to release blame and choose empathy. It's the quiet voice that says, "We are still family. We still belong to one another."

I didn't know it then, but that season planted the seed for everything I now believe about grace.

Reflection & Spiritual Insight

Looking back, I now see what I couldn't see through the eyes of that young girl riding the school bus from a hotel, hoping no one would notice her shame. **Grace was there all along**. It wasn't loud or obvious. It didn't swoop in and change our circumstances overnight. But it sustained us. It softened hearts. It made a way where there was none.

God's grace didn't remove the pain of my parents' divorce, but it transformed the way I understood it. It reshaped my identity. In a world that split into "before" and "after," grace was the through-line. It was a reminder that I was still held, still worthy, still seen.

2 Corinthians 12:9 says, *"My grace is sufficient for you, for my power is made perfect in weakness."* That verse became real to me not because I was strong, but because I wasn't. Because I was a child feeling invisible, torn between two households, carrying questions too heavy to say out loud. And yet, in my weakness, God revealed Himself as enough.

What's powerful about grace is that it rarely shows up in grand, cinematic moments. More often, it's the friend who doesn't judge you, the ride to Bible study that plants the seed of faith, the mother who finds a way when there is no way, the father who keeps driving toward you despite the distance.

Grace doesn't require the story to be resolved. It shows up in the tension, in the transition, in the "still figuring it out." That's what makes it divine. It's not something we earn. It's something we receive especially when we feel least worthy.

I came to see my parents through the lens of grace: not as heroes or villains, but as humans; flawed, tired, doing their best with what they had. That realization softened something in me. It healed me in places I didn't know were broken. It allowed me to love them both, and to see the miracle in their co-parenting, even in the absence of their marriage.

Grace is what transforms trauma into testimony. It doesn't change the facts of the past, but it changes how we carry them. It reminds us that brokenness isn't the end of the story. It's the place where God often begins.

Related Bible Stories or Characters

One of the most profound biblical stories that mirrors the emotional weight of family fracture and healing grace is the story of **Joseph**.

Joseph's life was marked by betrayal. Sold into slavery by his own brothers, falsely accused in Egypt, and imprisoned for years, his story is one of deep brokenness, abandonment, disappointment, and loss. Yet through every painful chapter, God's grace was at work behind the scenes, positioning Joseph for something greater than he could have imagined.

Like Joseph, I experienced a sense of exile; removed from the stability of a childhood home, sent into unfamiliar places, and forced to make sense of emotional wounds I didn't cause. But just as Joseph eventually saw God's hand guiding him, I too began to understand that grace was with me—not only to sustain me, but to transform me.

Joseph's turning point comes when he is reunited with his brothers—the same ones who betrayed him. In that moment, rather than seeking revenge, he extends grace. He tells them, *"You intended to harm me, but God intended it for good to accomplish what is now being done, the saving of many lives."* (Genesis 50:20)

This is the heart of grace: to look back on what tried to destroy you and declare that God used it to build something sacred.

In many ways, my parents, flawed as they were, offered each other the same kind of grace. They didn't erase the past, but they showed up in the present. They made sacrifices for me even while healing from their own wounds. And like Joseph, I learned to forgive not only them, but also the season itself. Because what once felt like exile became the foundation for a deeper faith, a clearer sense of compassion, and a calling to live and love in the gray.

Gray Space Exploration

Brokenness doesn't follow a clean arc. It's not a simple before-and-after narrative. It's layered, messy, and often unresolved. That's why grace matters most *in the gray*, the place where things can't be easily labeled "good" or "bad," "right" or "wrong."

My parents' divorce was not a singular event. It was a series of ripples that shaped every area of my life. There was no clear villain, no perfect victim. There was pain. There were choices. And there were consequences. But there was also love. Imperfect love. Tired love. Complicated love. And in the middle of it all was grace.

It was messy to feel both admiration and resentment. To attend private school one week and live in a hotel the next. To feel emotionally neglected and deeply loved by the same people. This was not a season that fit into neat spiritual platitudes or cultural expectations.

The gray space was learning to forgive without pretending I wasn't hurt. It was honoring my parents' sacrifices while grieving what I lost. It was finding faith in a God who allowed instability, yet never stopped showing up through community, opportunity, and unexpected provision.

This is the space where grace thrives, not by fixing everything, but by helping us hold tension without losing hope.

Grace doesn't demand that the story makes perfect sense. It just asks us to *stay open*, to healing, to perspective, to love that doesn't always look the way we expected.

Connection to Reader's Life

Maybe your brokenness doesn't look like mine. Maybe it came through a loss you couldn't speak aloud, a betrayal that still stings, or a season where life fell apart without warning. Maybe, like me, you've carried silent grief, wondering if anyone sees how hard you're trying to hold it all together.

You're not alone.

We all walk through gray seasons, moments where nothing makes sense, and everything feels heavy. In those moments, it's easy to feel unseen by others and even forgotten by God. But grace whispers something different. It says: *You are not the sum of your suffering.* You are still whole. You are still worthy. You are still deeply loved.

Take a breath and reflect: What were the moments that threatened to define you? Who or what helped carry you through? Can you trace the thread of grace, even if it was quiet, even if it was just enough to get through the day?

This chapter isn't about fixing brokenness. It's about honoring it. It's about recognizing that grace doesn't wait for you to be okay. It meets you in the mess and chooses to stay. Even when you're shattered, even when you feel unlovable, grace holds you together in ways you can't always see.

Let this be your reminder: You do not have to be whole to be held. You do not have to be healed to be loved. You do not have to have it all figured out to be walking in God's grace.

Practical Application

1. Breath Prayer for the Brokenhearted Inhale: *"Your grace is enough..."* Exhale: *"...even here."* Use this short prayer when you're overwhelmed or feel the weight of grief pressing in. It anchors your body and spirit in God's truth.

2. Mirror Moments Each morning, look into the mirror and speak one gentle truth over yourself. Examples:

- "I am allowed to grieve and grow."

- "My brokenness does not disqualify me."

- "God sees me even when I feel invisible."

3. Grace Journal Prompt Set aside time each week to reflect:

- Where did I feel broken this week?

- Who or what reminded me I wasn't alone?

- What small sign of grace showed up unexpectedly?

4. Scripture to Sit With Write 2 Corinthians 12:9 on a sticky note or card. Keep it near your workspace, mirror, or nightstand. Let it become a daily whisper to your heart: *"My grace is sufficient for you, for My power is made perfect in weakness."*

5. Reach for One Safe Soul You don't have to tell your whole story. But consider reaching out to one person who feels safe. Vulnerability invites grace to meet us through human connection.

Reflection Questions

1. When have you felt most broken in your life? What emotions surfaced in that season?

2. Can you identify moments where grace showed up, perhaps through people, timing, or inner strength?

3. What messages about suffering or weakness did you grow up believing, and how do they compare to the truth of 2 Corinthians 12:9?

4. How might your story change if you viewed your brokenness as a space for grace rather than shame?

5. Who in your life needs a reminder that they are not defined by what they've been through? How can you reflect God's grace to them?

Closing Blessing

May you come to see that your brokenness is not a barrier to grace, but an invitation. May the pieces you thought disqualified you become the very places God makes His presence known. When the world feels heavy, may you remember: you are not alone, and you are not beyond repair. God sees you. He holds you. He calls you whole even when you feel shattered. May grace meet you in the middle of the mess, and remind you that even here, especially here, you are deeply loved.

Amen.

Chapter Two

♥

If it is possible, so far as it depends on you, live peaceably with all."

Romans 12:18 (NRSV)

Chapter Summary

G race isn't always wrapped in resolution. Some relationships end without apologies. Some stories close without a final chapter. In this section, we explore the pain of unresolved endings, the ghost of a friendship that no longer exists, the ache of love unreturned, the conversations that never happened. When closure never comes, grace steps in as a healing balm.

This chapter explores how God's grace can meet us in that liminal space, not to tie everything up neatly, but to offer peace even when the outcome is incomplete. The gift of grace is not always reconciliation with others, but always restoration within ourselves.

Where Grace Met Me: Friendship Fracture & Rebuilding Trust

There was a time when I thought we'd be the kind of friends who aged together with ease. You know the kind, matching gray streaks in our braids, knowing glances across crowded rooms, kids who grew up calling each other "cousin" even though there was no blood between us. She wasn't just a friend; she was my *person*. The one I called after late-night heartbreaks and early-morning wins. The one who prayed me through panic attacks and sat beside me in church like we were born to share pews and secrets.

And then, she was gone.

Not literally, not in the dramatic way people sometimes exit. There was no blowout fight, no name-calling, no slammed doors. Just... quiet. Like someone turned the volume down on our friendship and forgot to turn it back up.

At first, it was subtle: a delay in texting back, missed calls that went unanswered, invitations declined without explanation. But over time, the silence thickened. I reached out. I asked if everything was okay. She said it was. But her absence said otherwise.

I would've preferred an argument, honestly. At least then I'd have something to hold. Something to fight through. But instead, I was left with nothing but questions, questions that echoed louder in the absence of answers.

I replayed conversations in my head, combed through text threads like a detective, searching for the moment I must've offended her, hurt her, failed her. But I couldn't find it. And that might've been the hardest part, not knowing what I did or didn't do. Just knowing that what once felt unbreakable had quietly broken, and I wasn't invited to the ending.

And still, I loved her.

That's the complicated thing about relationships that end without ceremony. You don't get to lay them to rest. There's no funeral. No closure. Just a living ghost who walks around in your memories, brushing up against your joy with the bittersweet reminder that they used to be part of it.

I carried that grief like a purse I never meant to bring. It hung at my side through every milestone, every hard day, every celebration that I instinctively wanted to share with her. And for a while, I did what many of us do, I told myself I was over it, that it didn't matter, that I was fine. But grief has a way of leaking out. It showed up in unexpected ways, like when I saw someone else laugh the way she used to, or when a sermon touched a nerve I thought had healed.

I asked God for resolution. I asked Him to bring her back. Or at the very least, to give me a clear reason why she left. But heaven stayed quiet. And that silence, that divine stillness, became part of my healing.

Because eventually, I stopped asking "Why did she leave?" and started asking, "What do You want me to learn here?"

That's when grace began to stir.

Not the shiny kind of grace that ties things up in a neat bow. But the slow, unglamorous kind, the kind that teaches you how to live with the ache. How to soften the sharp edges of resentment without pretending they never cut you. How to honor what was, even when what is feels like a betrayal of it.

Grace, in this case, looked like holding space for her memory without needing her presence. It looked like blessing her name in prayer, even as I wiped away the tears. It looked like trusting that closure is sometimes a luxury, but peace is always possible.

And then, one day, without warning, she messaged me. It wasn't dramatic. Just a "Hey, I've been thinking about you." My heart didn't leap. It ached. Because even in that moment, I knew better than to expect things to return to what they were. I responded with kindness, but without attachment. Because I had already done the work of letting go.

She didn't come back to stay. And I didn't need her to.

That's the miracle of grace. It allows us to release people without bitterness. It teaches us that reconciliation is beautiful, but not always necessary for healing. That sometimes, the work is not in rebuilding a bridge, but in trusting God to carry you across the gap.

Grace without closure is a holy act. It's choosing peace when your questions go unanswered. It's loving someone from afar, without needing them to understand how much they hurt you. It's forgiveness without fanfare. It's trust without resolution.

And it is enough.

Reflection & Spiritual Insight

There's a specific kind of heartbreak that doesn't come with a clear beginning or end. It doesn't make itself known through drama or confrontation. It comes quietly, like fog creeping in overnight, soft, but suffocating. That's what makes it so disorienting. When a friend drifts away without a word, when love fades without explanation, we're left holding not just grief, but confusion.

And in that confusion, many of us begin to spiral. *What did I miss? Why wasn't I enough? Was I ever as close to them as I believed I was?*

These questions don't just fracture our trust in others, they challenge our trust in ourselves, in our own discernment, even in God.

Because if God is love, why does love sometimes leave? If God is just, why don't we always get clarity?

These are not small questions. They are soul-deep, and they deserve gentleness. But here's the truth I've come to understand: grace is not always about restoration; sometimes it's about release.

We often equate grace with reunion. With the picture-perfect moment when someone comes back and says, *"I'm sorry."* And while that kind of healing is beautiful, it's not the only kind. In fact, some of the most powerful grace work happens when no apology ever comes. When the door doesn't swing back open. When the silence stays silent.

In those moments, grace isn't a conversation; it's a *posture*. It's what happens in your own heart when you decide that someone else's choices won't control your peace. It's what forms in the soil of abandonment when you let God plant something new. It's the sacred decision to let go, not because they deserve it, but because *you do*.

The Bible doesn't shy away from these gray relational spaces. In fact, one of the clearest examples of grace without closure is found in the life of Jesus. In John 6:66–67, after a particularly hard teaching, many of Jesus' disciples "turned back and no longer followed Him." They didn't argue. They didn't explain. They just left.

Jesus didn't chase them.

He turned to the twelve and asked, *"Do you also want to go away?"* (John 6:67). There was no bitterness, only invitation. Jesus knew that not everyone would stay, and He also knew that grace doesn't beg for love to return. It simply remains *available*.

That's what I'm learning to embody: grace that remains open, but not desperate. Grace that blesses even the ones who ghosted you. Grace that doesn't demand a reunion to validate your worth.

Because here's the holy paradox: you can be fully loving *and* walk away. You can grieve someone's absence *and* stop waiting for their return. You can release someone from the story without writing them as the villain.

That's grace.

And sometimes, sometimes, that kind of grace *is* the closure.

Related Bible Stories or Characters

When we experience broken or unresolved relationships, especially ones that end without warning, we often internalize the loss as failure. We wonder if it's our fault. We carry unanswered questions like stones in our pocket. Was it something we said? Something we missed? Why didn't they say goodbye?

And while those feelings are deeply personal, they're not unique. The Bible quietly echoes this pain. In the sacred pages of Scripture, nestled between the miracles and the victories, are the stories of people who were left. People who were betrayed. People who loved deeply and lost suddenly, without apology, without closure, without the satisfaction of knowing why.

And yet... grace still moved. Healing still happened. God still used the fragments.

Jesus and Judas: Grace in the Face of Betrayal

One of the most heart-wrenching examples of grace without closure is the story of **Jesus and Judas**. It's a story many of us have heard a hundred times, but when read through the lens of relational rupture, it cuts differently.

Judas wasn't a background character. He wasn't a vague name on the edge of the crowd. He was one of *the twelve*. Handpicked. Trusted. A man who walked beside Jesus, ate with Him, laughed with Him, witnessed miracles firsthand. He wasn't just part of the ministry; he was part of the inner circle.

And Jesus knew. He knew from the beginning that Judas would betray Him. Yet still, He chose him. Still, He welcomed him to the table. Still, He washed his feet the night before the betrayal. That image alone, the Son of God kneeling to cleanse the feet of the very man who would turn Him over to death, might be one of the most powerful acts of grace ever recorded.

And what's even more astonishing?

Jesus let him go.

He didn't beg him to stay. He didn't demand an explanation. He didn't try to fix what was clearly unraveling. He simply said, *"What you are about to do, do quickly."* (John 13:27)

That one sentence, quiet and loaded, speaks volumes about the way Jesus navigated human relationship. He didn't force reconciliation. He didn't try to control the outcome. He let Judas make his choice, and then He chose grace anyway.

Jesus didn't get closure. He got betrayal. And still, He went to the cross in love. Still, He laid down His life, not just for the faithful, but for the faltering. Not just for the ones who stayed, but for the one who left.

If Jesus can extend that kind of grace to someone who betrayed Him with a kiss, surely we can learn to offer grace to those who ghosted us without explanation, who disappeared from our lives when we needed them the most.

Paul and Barnabas: Grace in Disagreement

Another example, more subtle but just as profound, is the story of **Paul and Barnabas** in Acts 15.

Paul and Barnabas were ministry partners. Friends. Brothers in faith. They had traveled together, preached the gospel side by side, suffered together. Their bond was forged in fire, deep and purposeful.

But even they couldn't avoid conflict.

Their disagreement centered on John Mark, who had abandoned them on an earlier journey. Barnabas, ever the encourager, wanted to give John Mark another chance. Paul wasn't willing. Their dispute wasn't minor; it was sharp. So sharp, in fact, that the Bible says they parted company.

Just like that.

No big fallout scene. No apology letter. No tidy bow at the end of the chapter. Just two people who had once walked closely together... now walking in different directions.

And here's what's most telling: **Scripture doesn't judge either one of them.** It doesn't say Paul was right and Barnabas was wrong, or vice versa. It simply records the fact: the relationship changed. The ministry continued. And grace covered both journeys.

Later, we see hints that Paul's heart toward John Mark softened. In one of his final letters (2 Timothy 4:11), he tells Timothy, *"Get Mark and bring him with you, because he is helpful to me in my ministry."*

No dramatic reunion scene. No mention of Barnabas. Just quiet evidence that grace had done its work, even without a formal reconciliation.

That's the kind of grace many of us have to live into: the kind where there's no big moment of reckoning. Just a shift. A softening. A choice to move forward with love, even when the relationship itself doesn't come back around.

What These Stories Teach Us

What we see in both Jesus and Paul is the willingness to accept that not every relationship is meant to be forever, and that *God can still move in the spaces we don't fully understand.*

These stories remind us that grace is not about tying everything up neatly. It's about *trusting God with the loose ends.*

It's trusting that:

- **You don't have to hear "I'm sorry" to forgive.**

- **You don't have to be understood to choose peace.**

- **You don't have to stay connected to love someone from afar.**

These biblical figures weren't immune to the mess of human relationship. But they modeled a deeper truth: that *grace doesn't always need resolution to be real.*

If Jesus could release Judas with compassion... If Paul could part ways with Barnabas without animosity... Then maybe we can start to release our own expectations of closure. Maybe we can begin to believe that peace isn't found in perfect endings; it's found in trusting God with the unfinished ones.

Gray Space Exploration

There's a space we don't talk about enough.

It's not the space of rage, where emotions boil over into confrontation. It's not the space of forgiveness with a ribbon on top, where both parties sit down, talk it out, and hug it out.

No, this space is quieter. It's lonelier. It's filled with echoing questions, unsent messages, and the ache of conversations that never happened.

This is the *gray space* of relationships, the place between closeness and cutoff. It's the emotional purgatory we find ourselves in when someone walks away without explanation. When the silence is louder than any argument would've been.

And the truth is? That space is incredibly hard to live in.

We are storytelling creatures. Our brains crave beginnings, middles, and satisfying ends. We want to know why something happened. We want to assign blame or responsibility. We want to understand who was right and who was wrong. It makes us feel safe. It gives us the illusion of control.

But the gray space laughs gently at that need.

In my own life, I've learned this: there are people you will never get closure from. Not because you didn't deserve it. Not because you didn't try. But because they weren't capable of giving it. Emotionally. Spiritually. Sometimes even physically.

And grace? Grace is what shows up when closure doesn't.

Grace sits beside you on the couch when the phone doesn't ring. It doesn't rush in with answers, but it does hand you a warm blanket and a reminder: *"You are not alone in this liminal space."*

I remember scrolling through old photos one night, me and the friend I lost without warning. Our laughter caught in frozen frames. Birthdays. Road trips. Lazy Saturdays. I sat there staring at the faces we used to wear when the world made sense. And I cried. Not because I wanted to go back. But because I had finally allowed myself to grieve what would never be again.

Grief is part of grace.

That was the moment I realized: closure isn't a door someone else has to close for you. It's a decision to stop standing in the hallway, waiting.

It's saying to yourself: *"I may never get the answers I crave. But I will no longer wait for them to heal."*

That's where grace lives, in the choosing. In the release. In the fierce, trembling courage to carry on with a heart that is still tender, still open, still capable of loving again.

There's a holy kind of wisdom that comes from sitting in this gray space and not running from it. It's the kind of wisdom that reminds you life isn't binary. People aren't just heroes or villains. Endings aren't always evil. Some exits were necessary, even if they came wrapped in silence and confusion.

Sometimes, the people we miss were hurting too. Sometimes their silence wasn't about us. Sometimes it was.

We may never know.

But what we do know, what we can cling to, is that **God is not afraid of gray.** He is not uncomfortable with tension. He does His best work in the middle.

Grace is what lets us stay soft in the ambiguity. It's what whispers: *"Even if you never hear from them again, your story is still worth telling. Your heart is still worth healing."*

And when we offer that same grace to others, to the ones who left, to the ones who couldn't stay, we experience a quiet resurrection. Not a return of what was lost, but the birth of something new: Peace that no longer depends on other people's actions.

Freedom from needing a reason to let go. Permission to carry love forward, even if it no longer has a destination.

This is the gift of the gray space: it teaches us how to love without attachment. How to grieve without hardening. How to find God in the middle of a sentence that never got its period.

It's uncomfortable. But it's sacred.

And sometimes, it's the very place where we learn how to become whole.

Connection to Reader's Life

Maybe as you've been reading this, a name has quietly surfaced in your heart.

Maybe it's someone you loved fiercely and lost without ceremony. A friend who slowly faded out of your life. A mentor who distanced themselves when you needed their guidance the most. A person who once made you feel seen, then left you standing in the dark with no map and no explanation.

Maybe you've spent nights replaying your last conversation, wondering if you missed a signal, said the wrong thing, leaned in too far. Maybe you've felt the shame of reaching out one too many times, only to be met with silence that stings more than any spoken goodbye. Maybe you've cried over unanswered texts or smiled sadly at photos from a time when you both still knew how to belong to each other.

If so, I want to say something tender and true: *You are not the only one who's ever lived in the gray.*

We've all walked through seasons where someone we love disappears without a proper ending. We've all wrestled with the ache of an "almost" or the grief of a "what happened?" We've all had to hold the weight of a relationship that used to be safe, and now feels like a wound we're not sure how to wrap.

These moments can make us question our worth, our instincts, even our sanity. But you are not crazy. You are not broken. You are simply carrying the ache of something that mattered.

And here's the radical grace of it all: **you do not need their return to be whole. You do not need their closure to begin healing.**

You get to choose peace, even if they never give you permission.

You get to wake up tomorrow and decide, *"I will no longer define my worth by who stayed or who left. I will define it by the fact that I kept loving, even through loss."*

That's grace.

That's power.

That's healing.

So take a moment. Let your heart speak. Who are you still waiting on? What apology are you still hoping for? What explanation do you still crave?

And now, gently ask yourself: *What would it look like to stop waiting? To release them to God and trust that your story doesn't end here?*

Maybe they'll come back. Maybe they won't. But that's not the point. The point is that you are already loved. Already worthy. Already surrounded by grace.

You are allowed to honor the memory *and* move on. You are allowed to forgive without reconciling. You are allowed to create space in your heart for something new, something sacred, born from your own resilience.

So take the next breath. And the next. You don't need the answers to start walking toward peace.

You just need a little grace for yourself. And maybe today, that's exactly what God is handing you.

Practical Application / Tools for Grace

When closure isn't something you receive, you have to learn how to create healing on your own terms, with God's help. Here are five gentle, grace-centered tools to help you release, remember, and rebuild.

1. Write the Letter (and Don't Send It)

This is a sacred release. Sit down with paper or your journal and write the letter you never got to send. Say everything. The gratitude. The grief. The questions. The disappointment. The love.

Let it be messy. Let it be honest. Let it be healing.

Then pray over it. Tear it up. Burn it. Tuck it in a drawer. Whatever feels right.This practice is not about them; it's about *you* reclaiming your voice and choosing to stop holding what they left you with.

2. Create a Goodbye Ritual

When people leave without saying goodbye, it leaves us stuck in limbo. So we say goodbye for ourselves.

Light a candle. Read a psalm (Psalm 34 or 147 are beautiful choices). Place a small object, like a stone or flower, in a special place to symbolize release. Speak this aloud if you feel ready:

"I bless what was. I release what no longer is. I open my heart to what is to come."

Ritual gives your soul a chance to breathe and move forward.

3. Name the Grace

Take out your journal or phone and answer this: *Where did grace show up in that relationship?*

- Was it a lesson you learned?

- A boundary you finally recognized?

- A piece of yourself you reclaimed?

Even if the relationship ended painfully, grace might've still left you with a gift. Name it. Honor it. Let it remind you that even in endings, God is working.

4. Pray for Them (Yes, Even Now)

This isn't about spiritual superiority; it's about spiritual freedom. When you carry bitterness, it weighs down your spirit.

Offer this breath prayer when memories return or the ache flares up:

Inhale: *"God, I release them to Your care..."* Exhale: *"...and I reclaim peace for myself."*

You can even write a one-sentence prayer for their wholeness. You don't have to feel ready to forgive. You just have to feel willing to *not be stuck* anymore.

5. Bless Your Present Relationships

Sometimes we're so focused on who left, we miss the beauty of who stayed, or who is here now.

Make a list of three people who consistently show up for you in big or small ways. Text them. Write them a note. Thank them for their presence. Celebrate the relationships that are still alive and well.

It reminds your heart: *you are not alone, and love is still available to you.*

Reflection Questions

1. **Who in your life do you still feel emotionally tethered to, even if they're no longer present?** What feelings surface when you think about them? What do you wish you could say?

2. **How has the absence of closure impacted your sense of self-worth, trust, or identity?** Are there lies you've believed because of someone's silence? How might grace speak a different truth?

3. **Can you identify moments of grace that appeared even in the pain of disconnection?** Did God comfort you through someone else, give you clarity, or open a new path

as that door closed?

4. **What would "release" look like for you today?** Would it be a prayer, a boundary, a ritual, or simply choosing to stop replaying the story?

5. **Who are the people in your life right now that deserve more of your emotional attention and presence?** What could shift if you chose to invest in the love that's here rather than the love that left?

Closing Blessing

May you make peace with the unanswered questions.May you no longer need their apology to rest.May you stop waiting at doors that no longer open, and turn instead toward the wide, wild landscape of your own healing.

May the silence they left behind become a sacred hush where God speaks louder than their absence ever could.

May you find the strength to let go, not with bitterness, but with blessing. To whisper, "Thank you for what was," and "I release you from what will never be."

May your heart stay soft, even after the breaking. May your love deepen, not because of who stayed, but because *you stayed with yourself.*

And when the ache returns, as it sometimes will, may you remember this: You are not unloved just because they stopped loving you. You are not unworthy just because they didn't return. You are not forgotten. You are not invisible.

You are held. You are seen. And even here, in this strange, unclosed chapter, **you are still becoming whole.**

Amen.

Chapter Three

♥

*"Let anyone among you who is without sin be the first
to throw a stone at her."*

John 8:7 (NRSV)

Life rarely fits into the neat boxes we try to place it in. We want clarity, control, and clean lines, but more often, we find ourselves in the in-between. This chapter explores the discomfort and spiritual tension that arises when life doesn't offer clear answers, when we can't easily discern who's right or wrong, or when love and hurt show up in the same place. As a pastor's child raised in a world of moral absolutes, I was taught to follow the rules, to see people and choices in terms of good or bad. But life taught me otherwise.

Chapter Summary

This chapter invites readers into the sacred complexity of the gray spaces, those seasons where judgment gives way to empathy, and certainty is replaced with curiosity. Here, grace doesn't just visit; it takes up residence. Through personal stories and biblical insight, we'll examine how grace calls us to put down our stones and pick up compassion, how it thrives not in easy answers, but in honest tension.

Where Grace Met Me: From Rejection to Redemption

I used to believe that if you followed the rules, life would follow suit.

Growing up in a pastor's home, morality was more than a guideline; it was the law of the land. I knew which words were off-limits, which skirts were too short, and which questions were better left unasked. Things were simple. Right was right. Wrong was wrong. I found comfort in that certainty. It gave structure to a world that already felt shaky beneath my feet.

But then life happened.

I began to see the cracks in that clear-cut worldview when I noticed how much people were struggling behind their smiles, especially the ones who seemed to have it all together. The older I got, the more life peeled back the curtain. It wasn't just outsiders who were hurting. It was people in my own circle. My family. My friends. Me.

One of the most defining seasons of my life started not with a thunderclap of tragedy, but with the quiet, persistent ache of confusion.

My sister and I were born years apart. She was already navigating her own storms by the time I came along, bruised by life in ways I wouldn't understand until much later. But at the time, all I knew was that I longed for her affection and rarely received it. She was distant, sometimes cutting, always out of reach. And I... I was the annoying little sister who seemed to irritate her simply by existing.

I remember one Christmas when I was about ten. I had spent weeks picking out the perfect gift for her with the tiny budget my mom gave me, some glittery hair clips and a handwritten note promising to stay out of her room for the rest of the year. I wrapped it in sparkly paper and taped it meticulously, feeling hopeful. When she opened it, she barely looked up.

"Thanks," she mumbled flatly, tossing the note aside.

I laughed it off at the time. Told myself it didn't matter. But it did. I cried in the bathroom that night, trying to understand what I had done wrong. Why did she treat me like I was a nuisance? What had I done to deserve her coldness?

The truth? Nothing.

But I wouldn't learn that until years later.

At the time, I internalized her rejection as a reflection of my worth. I believed her distance meant I wasn't lovable. And so I worked harder. Tried to be perfect. Stayed out of trouble. Got straight A's. Smiled when I wanted to scream.

But inside, I was unraveling.

The hurt built up silently, like sediment in a riverbed, layer after layer of unanswered questions, misunderstood intentions, and quiet resentment. I never said how much her words stung. I never told her how often I cried after our conversations. I just kept showing up, hoping that one day she'd see me.

Years passed. We grew into women. Our lives moved in different directions. And then, without warning, something began to shift.

It wasn't one single moment. It was the accumulation of many small ones. Late-night phone calls. Inside jokes. Shared grief. Vulnerability sneaking its way in, uninvited but welcome. My sister began to show up, not perfectly, but honestly. And I began to let go, not of the memory of pain, but of the belief that it defined us.

We talked about our childhood for the first time like two survivors sorting through the same wreckage with different memories. She told me she had been hurting too, that my arrival felt like the final straw in a life already full of unmet needs and silent battles. Her rejection wasn't about me. It was about her.

And suddenly, things weren't so black and white anymore.

I didn't need her to be the villain to heal. I just needed to understand the truth behind her actions, and to offer the kind of grace I'd once prayed someone would offer me.

Looking back, I see how easily I could've carried that wound forever. It would've been simpler to label her as cruel, to hold her at a distance, to protect myself from the chance of further pain. But grace doesn't thrive in protection. It thrives in proximity. It meets us in the messy middle, in the gray.

Today, my sister is one of my best friends. She's my sounding board, my cheerleader, my partner in chaos and creativity. She's the person I call when I'm unsure, the person I text with my deepest doubts and wildest dreams. But we didn't get here by pretending nothing ever happened. We got here by being honest about the hurt and staying in the conversation long enough for healing to begin.

This is the gray space of grace: where people can be both hurting and hurtful, where love and wounds coexist, where relationships don't follow a script but still find their way to wholeness. It's not neat. It's not easy. But it's holy.

Reflection & Spiritual Insight

When I look back on my relationship with my sister, I no longer see it as a story of rejection; I see it as a masterclass in grace.

Because grace doesn't always look like reconciliation wrapped in a bow. Sometimes, it looks like discomfort. Like silence stretching between two people for years. Like deep breaths before hard conversations. Like forgiveness that arrives quietly, not with fireworks, but with a whisper: *"I see you. I know you were hurting. And I'm still here."*

Growing up, I clung to certainty. I needed things to be either/or, either you loved me or you didn't. Either you were kind or you were cruel. But grace taught me a new language, one fluent in *both/and*. My sister was both broken and beloved. Her words both hurtful and honest. Our relationship both painful and healing.

The more I studied Scripture, the more I realized that God's grace often met people in the gray.

Take the woman caught in adultery in John 8. She stood in the middle of a crowd that demanded justice, law, and judgment. According to the religious code, her fate was sealed. But Jesus didn't reach for a stone. He reached for understanding. He knelt in the dirt, perhaps to remind everyone where we all come from, and said, *"Let any one of you who is without sin be the first to throw a stone at her."*

What He offered that day wasn't just freedom for the woman. It was freedom for everyone present, freedom from the illusion of moral superiority, from the urge to cast blame without context, from the need to define people by their worst moments.

Jesus didn't ignore the sin. But He also didn't ignore the humanity.

That's what grace does. It holds the tension. It doesn't excuse harm, but it doesn't withhold love. It doesn't demand we forget, but it invites us to forgive. Grace acknowledges the mess and still calls us worthy. It chooses restoration over revenge. Curiosity over condemnation. Proximity over pride.

My sister taught me that.

And in return, God taught me this: if we're going to love like Christ, we have to learn to live in the gray.

We have to stop asking, *"Who's right?"* and start asking, *"Who's hurting?"* We have to stop clinging to certainty and start reaching for compassion. We have to stop drawing lines and start building tables.

Because grace isn't for the perfect; it's for the people brave enough to admit they're not.

The more I embraced that truth, the more I saw it ripple into other areas of my life. I found myself less reactive, more open. Less judgmental, more curious. I began to notice how often I used right/wrong language to protect myself from vulnerability. How often I clung to control when what I really needed was connection.

And slowly, I realized: the gray wasn't something to be feared. It was sacred ground.

The place where God's love meets human frailty. The space where healing begins, not because we figured it all out, but because we finally laid our weapons down. The middle ground where grace walks in, not to fix everything, but to help us keep walking.

Related Bible Stories or Characters

One of the clearest portraits of grace in a gray space is found in **John 8:1–11**, the story of the woman caught in adultery.

It was a setup from the beginning. The religious leaders weren't concerned with justice or morality. They wanted a spectacle. A trap. They brought the woman into the temple courts, placed her in the center of the crowd, and made her shame public. "The law says she should be stoned," they challenged. "What do you say?"

All eyes turned to Jesus. In that moment, the crowd wasn't looking for compassion; they were hungry for certainty. They wanted right and wrong. Guilty or innocent. Stone her or let her go. There was no room for nuance. No interest in her story. No questions about the man involved. Just judgment.

But Jesus didn't answer right away.

Instead, He bent down and wrote in the dust. He gave space to the tension. And then He spoke one sentence that cracked the entire system open: *"Let any one of you who is without sin be the first to throw a stone at her."*

Silence.

One by one, the stones dropped.

Jesus didn't deny that something wrong had occurred. But He reframed the moment, not as a legal matter, but a human one. He saw the woman, not as a category or cautionary tale, but as someone with a story. Someone worthy of dignity. Someone redeemable.

"Where are your accusers?" He asked.

"Gone," she replied.

"Then neither do I condemn you. Go now and leave your life of sin."

Grace didn't ignore the truth. But it also didn't weaponize it.

In that moment, Jesus modeled what it means to live in the gray. He chose empathy over condemnation. He reminded everyone that sin is not a ladder of comparison, but a common condition. And He extended a kind of grace that said: *You are more than your worst moment.*

That story mirrors so many moments in our own lives, the times when we're quick to label someone before knowing their context. When we hold people to the fire for things we ourselves have been forgiven for. When we forget that behind every action is a person. A soul. A story.

Just like the woman in John 8, my sister was living through things I couldn't see. Just like the accusers in that story, I was ready to cast judgment because it made me feel safer, more justified. But when I chose to lay my stone down, when I leaned into her humanity instead of her history, something sacred happened.

That's what grace does. It rewrites the ending. It lifts shame without ignoring truth. And it turns judgment into an invitation: *Come, be seen, be known, be loved anyway.*

Gray Space Exploration

There's a particular discomfort that comes when things refuse to make sense.

Our brains crave clarity. We want people to fit into tidy categories: good or bad, safe or unsafe, loving or toxic. We want to know who deserves forgiveness and who doesn't. But grace doesn't play by those rules. It shows up in the **blurred lines**, in the contradictions, in the places that make us question everything we thought we knew.

My relationship with my sister wasn't easy to name. She was neither hero nor villain. Our bond wasn't always warm or affirming. There were seasons when her words cut deeper than anyone else's. And yet, there was also love, real love, tucked beneath the sharp edges. It didn't make sense. It wasn't clean. It was gray.

And for a long time, I tried to escape the gray.

I tried to turn her into a story with a moral: the cold sister, the childhood wound, the emotional absence. It felt easier to carry my pain like a badge than to sit in the tension of loving someone who had also hurt me. But grace asked me to do something different.

Grace asked me to let the story stay unfinished.

To stop needing her to be one thing. To stop needing myself to be over it. To stop rushing toward resolution and instead learn how to live in the middle of the mess.

The truth is, most of life happens in the in-between.

We feel grief and gratitude at the same time. We carry forgiveness and frustration in the same breath. We love people who have disappointed us, and we disappoint people we deeply love.

And still, grace holds.

It holds when the apologies aren't perfect. It holds when the timing is awkward. It holds when the healing is slow, nonlinear, and uncomfortable.

The gray space is where grace earns its name, not by erasing the complexity, but by making us brave enough to stand inside of it without shutting down. It's where we learn to hold multiple truths without compromising compassion. It's where empathy expands. It's where our faith grows up.

Because anyone can extend grace when the story is simple.

But when the lines blur and the pain is tangled in love and the answers don't come wrapped in certainty? That's when grace becomes not just a virtue, but a lifeline.

Connection to Reader's Life

Maybe you're reading this and thinking of someone who's hurt you, someone who doesn't fit neatly into "forgivable" or "unforgivable." Maybe it's a parent who did their best but still left scars. A friend who ghosted you right when you needed them most. A sibling who made you feel invisible. Or maybe... it's you.

Maybe *you're* the one who doesn't know how to forgive yourself for the things you did before you knew better. Maybe you've spent years replaying a moment, a word, a mistake, wondering if it says something permanent about who you are.

If so, take a breath. You're not alone. And you are not your worst moment.

Grace sees the *whole* story.

It sees the heartbreak *and* the healing. The harm *and* the growth. The silence *and* the showing up. It doesn't require the full picture to start working; it enters right where you are, in the messy middle, with arms wide open.

You don't have to rush to label people as "good" or "bad" in order to feel safe. You don't have to resolve every tension to be at peace. Some relationships won't be tied up with a bow. Some wounds will never come with the apology you hoped for. And still, grace invites you to live open-hearted anyway.

Let this chapter be your permission to **stay soft in a world that wants you to go hard**. To love people who may never fully understand you. To forgive, not because they deserve it, but because you deserve to be free. To hold tension without losing yourself to bitterness or perfectionism. To trust that God is present even in situations that feel unresolved.

So ask yourself...

What if you didn't need all the answers to start healing?

What if grace isn't about understanding *why* something happened, but *how* you'll carry it?

What if the most sacred, soul-growing thing you do this year is **not fixing** what broke, but choosing to *see differently*, to love deeper, even in the uncertainty?

Because grace doesn't demand that you figure it all out. It only asks that you keep showing up.

Exactly as you are.

Especially when life doesn't make sense.

Practical Application / Tools for Grace

Living Gracefully in the Gray

We don't need to resolve the mess to invite God into it. Here are some tools to help you practice grace in the places where life refuses to give you clear answers.

1. The "Both/And" Journal

Once a week, write about a situation or relationship that feels complicated. Instead of labeling it good or bad, use "both/and" statements. Examples:

- *I am both hurt by what they did and open to healing.*

- *I am both confused and still choosing to trust God.*

- *I am both grieving and growing.*

Let yourself live in the tension without trying to resolve it.

2. Breath Prayer for the Gray Space

Use this breath prayer when you're overwhelmed by uncertainty or stuck in judgment.

Inhale: *God, meet me in the middle...* **Exhale**: *...with grace that holds both truth and love.*

Repeat it slowly, as many times as needed, until your shoulders drop and your heart softens.

3. Grace Filter Practice

The next time someone's behavior triggers confusion or frustration, pause and ask:

- What might I not be seeing about their story?

- What assumptions am I making?

- How would I respond if I believed they were doing the best they could?

This isn't about excusing harm; it's about opening the door to empathy.

4. Sit With the Unresolved

Choose one situation in your life that feels *unfinished*, a conversation never had, a closure never received. Light a candle, play calming music, and sit quietly with it. Say aloud: *"I release the need to understand everything. Grace is enough."*

Let the lack of clarity be holy ground.

5. Scripture to Keep Close

Write this on a card and place it where you'll see it:

"Let any one of you who is without sin be the first to throw a stone." – John 8:7

Let it remind you that grace starts not with certainty, but with surrender.

When you practice grace in the gray, you don't just change how you see others, you change how you hold yourself. These tools aren't about fixing what's messy. They're about giving yourself, and others, permission to be human, right here in the in-between.

Reflection Questions

Use these prompts in your journal, small group, or prayer time. Let them sit with you. Don't rush through the tension; they were made to hold it.

> 1. Where in your life are you currently sitting in a gray space, something that feels unresolved, uncertain, or emotionally

complicated?

2. Have you ever judged someone before learning their full story? What shifted your perspective, if anything?

3. Who in your life lives in a gray space for you right now? How might you begin to see them through the lens of grace, not perfection?

4. How have you expected yourself to be either "all healed" or "completely broken", instead of allowing space for the both/and?

5. What would it look like to stop trying to fix something, and instead, trust that grace can hold it as it is?

Closing Blessing

A Blessing for the In-Between

May you be gentle with yourself in the places that don't make sense. May you find the courage to stay present when clarity doesn't come quickly. May grace meet you not in your certainty, but in your surrender.

When the path feels murky, when the people you love confuse you, when the story doesn't resolve neatly, may you remember: God dwells in the gray, too. And He is not afraid of the mess.

May you put down your need to judge, to fix, to know everything, and pick up love, curiosity, and compassion instead.

You do not have to understand it all to be faithful. You only have to be willing to see through God's eyes. And in those eyes, you are still held. Still safe. Still beloved.

Amen.

Chapter Four

♥

"As far as the east is from the west, so far he removes our transgressions from us."

Psalm 103:12 (NRSV)

We often find it easier to believe that God has forgiven others than to believe He's forgiven us. But this verse gently, yet firmly, reminds us that when God says He has removed our sins, He means completely, irreversibly. There is no boomerang effect with divine grace. No "I forgive you, but..." lingering in heaven's vocabulary. The space between the east and the west? That's how far your past mistakes are from your redeemed identity in Christ. If God has let it go, why are we still carrying it?

Chapter Summary

We are often the last ones to receive the grace we so freely give to others. We beat ourselves up over past mistakes, spiral into shame over unmet expectations, and silently carry the burden of perfectionism. But grace isn't only meant to be extended outward; it must begin within. This chapter explores the painful but liberating journey of learning to extend compassion, forgiveness, and patience to the person staring back at you in the mirror.

The emotional tension here is internal, the kind of silent suffering that no one sees. It's the quiet self-condemnation that creeps into our thoughts when we fall short or falter. But grace? Grace interrupts that inner critic with the loving voice of God. This chapter reveals the spiritual truth that God's mercy doesn't come with conditions or quotas. It's freely given, even when we feel least deserving. And once we learn to receive it, we start to walk in a freedom that can transform everything.

Where Grace Met Me: Healing Beyond the Hurt

I remember a time in my life when self-grace felt like a foreign concept, like a language I never learned to speak. I was twenty years old, sitting in a cold hospital room with a clipboard in my lap and a consent form for a hysterectomy staring back at me. I had been in and out of medical offices for over a year, poked and prodded, labeled and re-labeled with conditions that had no clear answers. And now, a doctor, a well-meaning one, I suppose, was telling me this was the only option left. To give up on motherhood before I'd even had a chance to dream it fully.

But here's the twist. When I arrived on the day of the surgery, the nurse came out, clipboard in hand, looking puzzled. "There's been a problem with your insurance," she said softly. "They won't cover the procedure." And just like that, the surgery was canceled.

At the time, I didn't see God's hand in that moment. I saw inconvenience. I saw rejection. I saw a confirmation of what I already believed about myself, that I was broken, unworthy, and unlovable. I walked out of that hospital with an invisible scar that felt deeper than any incision could have been.

In the months that followed, I unraveled. Not all at once. It was more like a slow, subtle erosion of hope. I began making choices from a place of pain, falling into relationships that reflected my shattered self-worth. I dated men who already had families, almost like I was punishing myself, placing myself in proximity to the one thing I thought I couldn't have. I poured love into children who weren't mine, and silently grieved every time their mothers reminded me of that truth.

Looking back, I realize that I wasn't just grieving infertility, I was grieving identity. I had built so much of my self-worth around the idea of motherhood that when it was threatened, I felt I had nothing left to offer. I was chasing worthiness in all the wrong places. And I was doing it all while showing up for others, smiling through pain, offering support, giving grace... to everyone but myself.

Years later, after much healing, therapy, prayer, and growth, I can name what I couldn't name back then: I was drowning in shame. And shame has this way of disguising itself as humility. But shame isn't the same as conviction. Conviction draws us closer to God. Shame drives us into hiding. And I was deep in hiding, from others, from God, and especially from myself.

But grace, grace was still there. Quiet and patient. Like sunlight slowly pouring into a dark room. It came in the form of mentors who refused to give up on me, friends who spoke life over me, and scriptures that began to penetrate the hardened parts of my heart. It came when I finally allowed myself to believe that I didn't have to be perfect to be loved. That my worth wasn't tied to my ability to produce, succeed, or perform. That I was already enough.

There's a moment I'll never forget: I was alone in my room, journaling, tears streaming down my face as I wrote the words, "I forgive you." Not to someone else, but to myself. It was the first time I had spoken grace into the depths of my being. And something shifted. Not all at once. But just enough to let the healing begin.

Reflection & Spiritual Insight

It's a strange kind of irony, isn't it? That we're often the most unforgiving toward ourselves. We extend second chances to others, speak life into our loved ones, pray for mercy on behalf of friends, and yet, when it comes to our own flaws, failures, and fumbles, we become ruthless. There's a voice in our heads that sounds suspiciously familiar, always whispering, *"You should've known better... You've done it again... How could you?"*

But here's the truth that grace gently offers: **God is not asking us to be perfect. He is inviting us to be free.** And freedom begins with self-compassion.

In that hospital waiting room, I didn't yet know the theology of grace. But I knew the theology of shame. I had memorized it like scripture. I believed that every misstep disqualified me. That my unfulfilled dreams were evidence of divine punishment. I thought the delay in motherhood was a reflection of personal failure, not divine timing. I didn't realize then that grace isn't something we earn; it's something we *accept.*

God's grace is always extended, but it's not always received. Why? Because our inner narratives often get in the way. We tell ourselves that healing must be preceded by penance, that we must punish ourselves before we can forgive ourselves. But that's not how God works. **In the Kingdom, mercy comes before merit. Love precedes transformation.**

Psalm 103 is one of the most tender, grace-filled chapters in the Bible. It begins by reminding us of who God is, not just as a Creator, but as a *compassionate Father*. It tells us He is "slow to anger, abounding in love" (v. 8). That "He does not treat us as our sins deserve" (v. 10). That He "remembers we are dust" (v. 14). And that's the most beautiful part, He knows we are frail. He knows our humanity. And He loves us still.

So why is it so hard to love ourselves with that same softness?

Because self-grace requires surrender. It demands that we release our tightly held expectations, that we stop measuring our worth by outcomes, and that we open our clenched fists to receive the gift that's been waiting all along: *you are already loved.* Not "once you're healed," not "when you get it right", but right now, in your unfinished state.

Grace doesn't just excuse your imperfections; it **embraces them.** And not in a permissive way, but in a redemptive one. God doesn't overlook your flaws; He invites them into His presence so He can heal them.

And here's the spiritual kicker: **you can't fully extend grace to others if you haven't first received it for yourself.** That's why Jesus said, "Love your neighbor *as yourself.*" If your internal voice is harsh, judgmental, and merciless, then inevitably, that posture spills out. But when you learn to be gentle with your own soul, you'll find yourself extending that same gentleness to others, effortlessly, sincerely, and freely.

Grace is not self-indulgence. It's not denial. It's divine alignment.

It's looking in the mirror and saying, "I am not my worst moment. I am not my biggest failure. I am not beyond redemption." It's trusting that if God calls you forgiven, then you must not keep labeling yourself guilty.

And here's the beautiful, upside-down, Spirit-led truth: **The more you practice self-grace, the more you become who God designed you to be.** Not weaker, not lazier, but softer, stronger, freer. Because self-grace doesn't lower the standard; it *raises your capacity to meet it with joy instead of shame.*

Related Bible Stories or Characters

When it comes to the concept of self-grace, few biblical figures illustrate the tension between guilt, redemption, and restoration quite like *Peter*.

Peter was bold, passionate, and loyal, until he wasn't. In one of the most painful and raw moments of the New Testament, Peter denies Jesus three times on the night of His arrest. This wasn't just a minor slip-up. This was a complete collapse under pressure, a betrayal from someone in Jesus' inner circle.

Can you imagine the weight of that failure?

Luke 22:61 tells us that after Peter's third denial, "the Lord turned and looked straight at Peter." That moment must have shattered him. Scripture says Peter "went outside and wept bitterly." Those weren't casual tears. That was soul-deep sorrow, the kind of grief that makes you want to disappear. The kind of shame that can make you question your entire identity.

Peter had been told he was the rock upon which the church would be built, and now he was just rubble. Or so he thought.

But here's where grace shows off.

After Jesus' resurrection, in John 21, we see an intimate, redemptive moment unfold. Jesus meets Peter on the shore. He's not angry. He's not cold. He doesn't throw Peter's failure in his face. Instead, He cooks him breakfast.

Let that sink in.

Before restoring Peter's position, Jesus nourishes him. Before giving him purpose, He gives him presence.

Then, three times, mirroring the three denials, Jesus asks, "Do you love me?" And three times Peter says yes. Jesus doesn't just forgive Peter. He reaffirms him. He re-calls him. He commissions him. *Feed my sheep*, He says. *Lead anyway.* Love anyway. Begin again.

That is the power of self-grace. It's knowing you've messed up... and choosing to rise anyway because God has already declared you forgiven. It's letting Christ's mercy become the louder voice in your life than your own self-condemnation.

Peter's story reminds us that failure isn't final in God's eyes. That restoration is real. And that sometimes, the only thing standing between you and the life you're meant to live... is your willingness to forgive *yourself*.

If Jesus reinstated Peter, if He called him still worthy to lead, still chosen to love, still trusted with purpose, then how dare we cancel ourselves over the places we've fallen short?

Gray Space Exploration

Self-grace lives in one of the murkiest, most misunderstood corners of our emotional and spiritual lives. It's the kind of grace that feels too indulgent for the church pew, too soft for a boardroom, and too foreign for the way many of us were raised. Most of us were taught how to repent, how to serve, how to strive, but not how to rest in mercy when the mirror feels like an accusation.

This is the gray space: the emotional no-man's land between ac-countability and self-condemnation.

We're told to be responsible, to own our mistakes, to do better, and all of that is holy work. But where does that leave us when we've done the work and still feel unworthy? Where do we go when we've apologized, grown, evolved, and yet still replay the same regrets in our minds like a broken record?

Grace doesn't live in the black-and-white extremes of *"I'm either good or I'm a failure."* It lives in the blur, the *both/and.* You can be both healing and still hurting. You can be a work in progress and still be wildly loved by God. You can acknowledge where you've fallen short without living your life as if you're forever in debt to your past self.

One of the messiest parts of self-grace is navigating that inner nar-rative that says you must keep paying for your mistakes. That you haven't suffered enough. That you can't move forward until you've reached some unspoken level of spiritual performance.

But grace doesn't work like a transaction. It's not earned through suffering. It's received through surrender.

And that's uncomfortable.

It's much easier to believe we're still unworthy than to believe God's love covers even the parts of us we try to hide. The gray space is trusting that God doesn't see us through the lens of failure, but through the lens of future. He sees the whole story. He knows the *why* behind the *what.* And even though He doesn't excuse our brokenness, He wraps it in mercy. He redeems it. He uses it.

In this in-between space, this emotional wilderness, we must ask ourselves: **What does it mean to live as someone God has already**

forgiven? That's where self-grace begins to bloom. Not in perfect resolution, but in the soft soil of release.

Connection to Reader's Life

Maybe you've been carrying something for years, an old regret, a missed opportunity, a failure that still plays like background music in your quiet moments. Maybe it was a season where you were lost, overwhelmed, bitter, reckless. Maybe it was a decision you made that you wish you could go back and undo. Or maybe, it wasn't just one moment, it was a slow erosion of self-worth, the kind that happens when you keep shrinking yourself for the comfort of others, or pretending you're okay when you're not.

You're not alone.

We all carry internal bruises, some visible, most hidden. And yet, so many of us walk through life with an unspoken belief: *Everyone else deserves grace... except me.* But friend, grace doesn't have exceptions. There's no fine print that excludes you.

Let's pause here.

What would it look like if you stopped punishing yourself? What if the voice in your head that replays every flaw was replaced with God's voice, the one that says, *You are my beloved... in you I am well pleased* (Luke 3:22)? What if healing started not with fixing yourself, but with *forgiving* yourself?

Here's the truth: you are not disqualified by your doubts, your detours, or even your darkest moments. Grace isn't scared of your past. And God is not waiting for you to get it all right before He wraps you in love. He's already here. Already extending His hand. Already whispering, *There's more to your story.*

This chapter is for the high achiever who is exhausted by her own expectations. For the man who can't stop replaying the thing he didn't say or the thing he did. For the mother who thinks she's not doing enough. For the person who keeps asking, *Why can't I move on?*

Self-grace doesn't erase the past. It reframes it. It says, *Yes, that happened. And yes, you're still worthy of love, healing, and forward movement.*

Let this be your invitation to breathe a little easier. To unclench your heart. To stop rehearsing shame and start embracing mercy.

God is not keeping score. He's writing a story.

And grace? Grace is the ink.

Practical Application / Tools for Grace

Self-grace isn't just a mindset; it's a daily practice. Like any spiritual discipline, it takes intentionality. But the good news? Grace doesn't require perfection. It only requires presence. Here are some soul-nurturing tools to help you soften toward yourself and begin walking in the gentle power of God's grace for *you*.

1. The Mirror Practice: Speak What God Sees

Each morning, look yourself in the eye, literally. Stand in front of a mirror and speak one truth over yourself. Not a flattery. A *truth*. Something that reflects how God sees you.

- "I am forgiven."

- "I am not my mistakes."

- "I am growing, and growth takes time."

- "God delights in me, even now."

Say it out loud. Say it until your body starts to believe it.

2. Breath Prayer for Self-Compassion

When anxiety or self-judgment starts to rise, anchor yourself with a breath prayer:

- **Inhale:** "Your grace is enough..."

- **Exhale:** "...even for me."

Repeat this slowly, letting each word land in your body. This sacred pause can become your reset button when self-criticism takes over.

3. Write a Letter to Yourself

This is one of the most healing tools I've ever practiced. Sit down, and write a letter to the version of you who felt the most unworthy. The 19-year-old who thought her body had betrayed her. The tired mom who felt like she was failing. The younger you who did the best she could with the tools she had.

Speak to her with the same gentleness you'd give a child. Say what you wish someone had said to you back then. Then read it aloud. Cry if you need to. Let it wash over you like grace.

4. Create a "Grace Jar"

Every time you mess up, miss a deadline, overreact, or fall short, write it down, fold it up, and put it in the jar. Once a week, open the jar and read each slip. But instead of judgment, speak a word of grace over each one:

- "Still loved."

- "Still worthy."

- "Still growing."

This simple act retrains your spirit to respond to imperfection with love instead of shame.

5. Sit with Psalm 103

Don't just read it; *soak* in it. Write it in your journal. Highlight the lines that make your heart stir. Meditate on verse 14: **"For He knows how we are formed, He remembers that we are dust."** God knows how fragile we are. He doesn't expect perfection; He expects honesty.

Reflection Questions

1. **Where in your life do you struggle most to offer yourself grace?** Think about situations where you're quick to judge yourself or hold on to guilt. What would it look like to meet those areas with compassion?

2. **What internal narrative have you believed that keeps you from embracing self-grace?** Are there stories you've told yourself, maybe for years, that it's time to release?

3. **Can you name a time when God extended grace to you, even when you felt undeserving?** Reflect on how that moment shaped your view of Him, and yourself.

4. **What would change in your daily life if you truly believed God's mercy covers *you*, too?** How would you speak to yourself? Treat your body? Approach your dreams?

5. **What's one step you can take this week to practice self-compassion?** Maybe it's resting when you feel pressure to push. Maybe it's journaling, speaking kindly to yourself, or finally letting go of something God already forgave.

Closing Blessing

May you remember, even now, that you are not your worst decision, your biggest regret, or the voice of shame that tries to haunt your quiet moments.

May the weight of perfection be lifted from your shoulders, and may you finally breathe in the truth that God's love is not performance-based; it is permanent.

When you look in the mirror, may you see not your flaws, but your Father's fingerprints, etched into your being, marked with mercy.

May you walk gently with yourself, knowing that growth takes time and that healing is not linear.

And on the days when you feel least deserving, may you dare to whisper: *"Even here, even now... I am still worthy of grace."*

You are held. You are healing. You are His.

Amen.

Chapter Five

♥

"The Lord is near to the brokenhearted, and saves the crushed in spirit."

Psalm 34:18 (NRSV)

There are moments that press so heavily on the soul, we begin to believe we've been forgotten. When silence echoes louder than any comfort, and hope feels more like a distant memory than a promise, we ask ourselves: *Where is God in all of this?* In these moments, grief-stricken, weary, and aching for understanding, grace does not roar. It whispers. It hides in the small things. In the quiet presence of a friend, in the steady breath we didn't know we had the strength to take, in the sunrise we didn't think we'd live to see. Grace doesn't always show up in the form we expect. But it always shows up.

Chapter Summary

This chapter explores the emotional and spiritual tension we experience when grace feels missing. It's about the hollow spaces left after disappointment, the confusion when prayers feel unanswered, and the heaviness that comes from spiritual silence. Many of us know what it's like to beg for divine intervention and be met with what feels like abandonment.

But what if grace isn't always loud or immediate? What if it doesn't come to *fix* things but rather to *carry* us through them? This chapter invites readers to recognize the hidden forms of grace that often arrive through sorrow itself. It is in the very absence we fear most that God is doing some of His deepest work. Grace, even when imperceptible, is never absent.

Where Grace Met Me: The Silent Grief

There are few things more delicate than hope, the kind that tiptoes in after years of aching, the kind you barely let breathe for fear it might vanish. For me, that fragile hope came wrapped in two pink lines. After years of health challenges, doctors' visits, invasive procedures, and warnings that I may never conceive, I had almost made peace with the idea that motherhood might not be part of my journey. But then, against every odd and every prediction, I became pregnant.

It was nothing short of miraculous. And so, I did what most hopeful hearts do: I celebrated. I shared the news earlier than some might recommend, unable to contain the joy I thought had been stolen from me. I dreamed out loud. I imagined baby names, nursery colors, little shoes and lullabies.

But then, without warning, hope slipped through my fingers.

The ultrasound was inconclusive, the technician silent. The room was filled with the kind of quiet that tells you something is wrong before the words catch up. I clung to the idea that maybe it was just too early, that perhaps the heartbeat would come later. But days later, I woke up in a pool of blood, and I knew. The life I had prayed for, fought for, was gone.

There is a particular kind of grief that comes with pregnancy loss, especially when that pregnancy felt like divine redemption. I was not only mourning the child I had never met, I was mourning the part of me that dared to believe again. The betrayal was more than physical; it felt spiritual. I questioned everything. Why would God open my womb only to let it empty? Why would He tease my heart with possibility, only to replace it with pain?

I remember staring at the ceiling in the middle of the night, tears soaking into my pillow, asking God questions He never answered. My faith, once my anchor, felt more like a weight I was dragging behind me. Worship songs felt hollow. Scripture felt far away. Prayer felt like speaking into a void. Grace? I couldn't find it. I couldn't feel it. And honestly, I didn't want it if this was what it looked like.

To make things worse, no one knew how to sit with me in my sorrow. Friends stayed silent, unsure of what to say. Some avoided me altogether. My husband and I grieved differently, he was quiet, inward, while I was loud and unraveling. We didn't know how to hold each other in a grief we couldn't understand ourselves.

I felt invisible. And deeply alone.

And yet, somehow, I kept breathing.

Grace didn't come in a grand, cinematic gesture. It wasn't in the form of answered prayers or comforting words. Instead, it came in the unlikeliest ways. It came in a cup of tea left at my bedside by a friend who didn't ask questions. It came in the warmth of sunlight spilling across the kitchen table one morning when I thought I couldn't get out of bed. It came in the simple act of a neighbor checking the mail for us, the soft murmur of my husband whispering "we'll try again," even when I wasn't ready to hope.

Eventually, I stopped asking God *why* and started asking *where*.

Where are you in this pain? Where are you when the world feels shattered? Where are you when the prayers are met with silence?

And that's when I began to notice, He had been there all along. In every quiet mercy, in every mundane kindness, in every act of survival. He hadn't stormed in to rescue me from the grief. He had simply taken a seat beside me and waited for me to feel Him again.

Months later, I would become pregnant once more. This time, we held the news closer. I whispered hope instead of shouting it. I prayed cautiously. I moved slowly. Even as each ultrasound revealed a growing child, I found it difficult to trust. It wasn't until I held my son in my arms, warm, crying, and impossibly real, that I let the tears of joy flow freely.

That moment, the weight of his tiny body on my chest, was grace embodied. It was not a replacement for the child I lost.

It was not a transaction to make the pain "worth it." It was something different. Something deeper. A reminder that grace does not erase the void but sometimes, just sometimes, it grows something beautiful beside it.

Even now, years later, when the sting of that loss creeps back in, I return to that moment and remember: grace never left. It just changed forms.

Reflection & Spiritual Insight: The Hidden Language of Grace

Looking back on that season of loss, I now understand something I couldn't see at the time: grace doesn't always look like comfort. Sometimes, it looks like survival. Sometimes, it looks like breathing through the ache, showing up when your heart is splintered, and choosing not to give up even when your faith has gone silent.

We often expect grace to feel warm, to come in like a balm to our wounds. We want the neat ending, the tidy resolution, the silver lining we can wrap into a testimony. But grace isn't always neat. It's not always obvious. Sometimes, it wears the face of confusion. Sometimes, it sounds like unanswered prayers. Sometimes, it *feels* like absence, but it is anything but.

There's a sacredness to the silence of God. In those moments when heaven feels quiet, it's not because God has turned His face away. It's because something deeper is taking root. The silence is not abandonment; it's invitation. Invitation into a faith that isn't propped up by circumstances or emotions. Invitation into trust that exists without guarantees. That's the kind of faith that births resilience. And that's the kind of grace that changes you from the inside out.

I think often of Jesus in the Garden of Gethsemane. The Son of God, sweating blood, crying out, "My Father, if it is possible, let this cup pass from Me..." (Matthew 26:39). Even Jesus, in His most human moment, pleaded for a different path. And yet, He wasn't spared from suffering. He was *strengthened* to endure it.

That's what grace does. It doesn't always remove the burden. But it gives us the strength to carry it.

Psalm 34:18 says, "The Lord is close to the brokenhearted and saves those who are crushed in spirit." I used to read that verse as a promise of intervention. Now, I see it as a whisper of presence. God may not always deliver us *from* the pain, but He is always in it with us. Crushed in spirit doesn't mean abandoned; it means *accompanied*.

I didn't recognize grace at the time because I was looking for it in the big things. The miracle. The healing. The answers. But grace was working in the micro-moments: the steadying breath, the friend who texted without knowing why, the ability to get out of bed when I didn't want to. That was grace. That was God.

There's a passage in 2 Corinthians 1:3-4 that says, "Praise be to the God and Father of our Lord Jesus Christ, the Father of compassion and the God of all comfort, *who comforts us in all our troubles, so that we can comfort those in any trouble with the comfort we ourselves receive from God.*" That verse has taken on new meaning for me. The grace I received, quiet, raw, imperfect, is now the grace I offer. And that offering is not born out of resolution but of redemption.

Even now, grace continues to teach me how to sit with others in their grief without rushing to fix it. It reminds me to stop offering answers when presence will do. It whispers, *"Stay."* Just stay. Stay with them. Stay with God. Stay in the moment, even if it hurts. Because grace is there too.

If you're in a season that feels dry, heavy, silent, know this: God's silence is not a lack of love. It is often the sacred space where your roots grow deeper, your faith stretches wider, and your heart becomes strong enough to hold both sorrow and joy at once.

Grace is not gone. It's just growing in the dark.

Related Bible Stories or Characters: Job & Hannah – Finding Grace in the Silence

When we talk about grace in the face of silence, no biblical figure speaks more profoundly to that experience than **Job**.

Job was a man who "was blameless and upright; he feared God and shunned evil" (Job 1:1). By all appearances, his life was a model of favor. And yet, in a matter of moments, he lost everything, his wealth, his children, his health. The people around him were quick to blame, to theologize, to analyze his suffering. But Job didn't need analysis. He needed presence. He needed grace.

What's astonishing about Job's story is that for most of the book, God is silent. Job cries out in anguish, laments the day of his birth, and pleads for understanding, but heaven doesn't immediately respond. And when God finally does speak, He doesn't offer a tidy explanation. Instead, He offers perspective: a vast, mysterious view of divine sovereignty that reminds Job that he was never alone. Grace didn't come in the form of answers. It came in the form of *relationship*.

Job's story reminds us that we don't always get the "why." But we are never without the *Who*.

And then there's **Hannah**, the mother of the prophet Samuel. For years, she lived under the heavy burden of infertility. She was mocked, misunderstood, and deeply grieved by her inability to conceive. Her womb was empty, but so was her spirit. She wept bitterly before the Lord (1 Samuel 1:10), pleading not just for a child, but for a sense of divine remembrance.

The beauty of Hannah's story isn't just in the eventual birth of her son; it's in the moment she poured out her soul and was met with compassion. Eli, the priest, at first mistook her silent prayer for drunkenness. But when he realized the depth of her sorrow, he blessed her. And that small moment, a human gesture of care, restored her hope.

Before her prayer was ever answered, grace began to work in her countenance. Scripture says that after she prayed, "her face was no longer downcast" (1 Samuel 1:18). Grace changed her even before her circumstances changed.

Both Job and Hannah show us that the silence of God is not the absence of God. They teach us that grace is not always loud, not always fast, not always easy. Sometimes, it comes in the weeping. Sometimes, it comes in the waiting. And sometimes, it comes in the simple know-ing that we are not forgotten.

These biblical stories echo our own. When we find ourselves staring into silence, pleading for relief, feeling unseen or unheard, we can remember: grace is not gone. It's forming something within us. Some-thing holy. Something lasting.

Gray Space Exploration: When There's No Bow on the Story

We don't talk enough about the middle.

We like testimonies that have endings, the kind where things re-solve, where the miracle comes just in time, where we can look back and say, *"Ah, now I see what God was doing."* But what about the in-between? The blurry stretch of time where the pain is real, the answers are absent, and the grace we believe in feels like a rumor from someone else's life?

That's the gray space.

This chapter lives here, in that murky, unpolished place where healing hasn't arrived, and faith doesn't always feel like enough. It's the tension between *what we believe about God* and *what we experience in the moment.*

In the aftermath of miscarriage, I wanted to tie it all up into a redemptive narrative. I wanted to find purpose in the pain, to point to something beautiful rising from the ashes. But the truth was: it just hurt. No explanation softened it. No spiritual platitude held weight. And for a long time, that felt like failure. Like I was doing grief, and faith, wrong.

But grace whispered something different.

Grace invited me to stop needing resolution in order to rest. Grace said, *"You don't have to be okay to be held."*

The gray space is messy. It's full of contradiction. I was grateful to be alive and angry to be suffering. I trusted God and questioned Him. I felt deeply loved and completely alone, all at the same time. And rather than trying to choose one side or the other, grace allowed me to feel it all.

We're not meant to sort our suffering into tidy categories of "good" or "bad," "blessed" or "forsaken." Life doesn't work that way. God doesn't either. Grace lives in the nuance. It lives in the breath between sobs. In the half-hearted prayers. In the silence between miracles. In the vulnerability of still showing up when your heart isn't sure it believes anymore.

And here's the thing about the gray space; it's not the absence of faith. It's where real faith is formed.

Because believing in grace when you *feel* it? That's easy.

But believing in grace when it feels a million miles away? That's holy.

So if you're in the middle, between the loss and the healing, the prayer and the answer, the ache and the restoration, this is your reminder: the gray is not a failure of faith. It's the sacred ground where grace takes root.

Connection to Reader's Life: Grace in

Your

Silence

Maybe your story doesn't involve miscarriage or infertility. Maybe your loss looks different. Maybe it came in the form of a job you desperately needed but didn't get. A relationship that ended with no closure. A dream that felt so aligned with God's plan that you still can't understand why it never came to pass. Or maybe it's something harder to name, a general heaviness, a fog of disappointment you can't quite shake, a spiritual exhaustion that's been building for years.

Whatever your pain looks like, I want to say something clearly: **you're not crazy for wondering where grace is.**

You're not faithless because you've doubted. You're not weak for feeling weary. You're not alone in the question marks that hang over your prayers.

You are human.

And in your humanity, you are held.

There will be seasons when you can't feel God, when your faith feels more like obligation than intimacy. Seasons when you show up to church, nod through the songs, read the verses, and feel nothing. That doesn't disqualify you. That doesn't make you unworthy. It doesn't mean grace has left.

It just means you're in the gray.

And maybe, just maybe, this chapter has found you at the exact moment you needed to hear: *You don't have to feel grace to be wrapped in it.*

Take a moment to look back, not for resolution, but for *remnants*. What were the tiny kindnesses that helped you keep going? Was there someone who showed up without needing you to explain? A moment of stillness that calmed your racing thoughts? A deep breath that felt like a miracle in itself?

Grace lives there.

You are not alone in your silence. You are not forgotten in your waiting. And this moment, this breath, is proof that grace has carried you further than you know.

You don't need to rush into healing. You don't have to pretend the silence doesn't bother you. Just keep breathing. Keep noticing. Keep hoping. Even if it's a faint whisper.

Grace has not left you.

It is growing something new, quietly, gently, invisibly, for now.

Practical Application / Tools for Grace: Practices for When Grace Feels Far Away

When grace feels absent, we don't need grand gestures; we need grounding. We need sacred pauses, soul-whispers, and small ways to tether ourselves back to what is true. Here are gentle tools to help you stay open when your heart feels closed, and keep breathing when belief feels brittle.

1. The "Even Here" Breath Prayer

Use this breath prayer when your thoughts are spinning or your heart feels heavy.

- **Inhale:** "God, you are near..."

- **Exhale:** "...even here."

Repeat it slowly, letting the words drop down from your mind into your body. Say it in the shower. Say it while driving. Say it when you don't believe it yet. This is not a magic spell. It's a lifeline, a way to stay connected in the silence.

2. A Grace Noticing Journal

Each evening, jot down *one* way grace may have shown up that day, even if it was tiny, even if it felt like nothing.

Examples:

- "The barista smiled at me when I was having a terrible morning."

- "I cried in the car and didn't feel ashamed about it."

- "Someone texted me just to say they were thinking about me."

These small entries become a breadcrumb trail when you feel lost.

3. Light a Candle for the Silence

Set aside five minutes to light a candle and do nothing but sit in God's presence. You don't have to speak. You don't have to feel anything. Just sit. Let the flame remind you that even when your soul feels dark, light is still present. Grace is still flickering.

4. Create a "Held" Playlist

Music can hold what words can't. Curate a playlist of songs that feel honest, soothing, or even raw. Include songs of lament *and* songs of hope. Let the music hold you when you can't hold yourself.

5. Ask Someone to Pray When You Can't

If prayer feels impossible, ask a trusted friend to pray on your behalf. Tell them, "I don't have the words right now, can you carry this for me?" Grace often shows up through the people willing to kneel when we no longer can.

None of these practices require you to "feel better." That's not the goal. The goal is presence. Stillness. Openness. The kind of small, sacred acts that make room for grace to move, even in the silence.

Reflection Questions

1. **When was the last time you felt distant from grace or from God?** What were the circumstances, and how did you respond emotionally or spiritually?

2. **Can you remember a time when grace showed up in a way you didn't recognize at first?** What did it look like in hindsight?

3. **How do you usually respond to spiritual silence?** Do you push through, withdraw, get angry, numb out, or something else?

4. **What small practices help anchor you when you feel lost or unseen?** Are there people, places, or rituals that remind you you're still held?

5. **If grace were a person sitting beside you in your current season, what might it say to you right now?** What would you want it to whisper into your weariness?

Closing Blessing

May you know, deep in your bones, that grace is not gone.

Even in the silence, even in the sorrow, even when the answers don't come, you are not alone.

May the God who whispers through the stillness meet you where words fail. May you find comfort in the quiet presence that does not demand performance, only permission, to grieve, to doubt, to rest.

May your tears be holy, your breath be sacred, and your story be wrapped in something bigger than explanation.

And when you cannot find grace, May grace find *you*.

Again and again. Always.

Amen.

Chapter Six

♥

"Truly I tell you, just as you did it to one of the least of these who are members of my family, you did it to me."

Matthew 25:40 (NRSV)

Grace is not passive. It's not just a gentle word whispered in prayer or a feeling we receive when life finally calms down. Grace moves. It steps into discomfort. It leans into interruptions. It says, *"Yes, I'll help,"* even when it would be easier to walk away. Grace puts on shoes, rolls up its sleeves, and shows up when love feels inconvenient or undeserved. It isn't loud or flashy; it's the quiet decision to forgive, the small act of kindness that breaks through someone's bad day, the moment you choose compassion over judgment. This chapter is an invitation to move, to let grace stretch beyond theory and take up space in your daily choices.

Chapter Summary

This chapter explores the practical side of grace, the grace that doesn't just sit in your heart but extends through your hands. This is where grace becomes action, not just sentiment. It's easy to understand grace when we're on the receiving end, especially during moments of deep need. But what happens when we are called to *give* grace in real time? When someone cuts us off in traffic, when a family member speaks in anger, when a coworker fails to pull their weight, what does grace look like *then*?

We'll dive into the emotional and spiritual tension that arises when we're called to embody grace instead of merely understanding it. This chapter will highlight the power of small, ordinary moments and how they can become sacred ground. We'll explore stories where grace wasn't the easy choice, but it was the right one, and how those decisions rippled outward in powerful ways. Grace in action reminds us that transformation doesn't always come from grand gestures. Sometimes, it's found in a grocery store checkout line, a text message of forgiveness, or a decision to stay in the conversation just a little longer. When grace becomes a verb, it becomes a witness to the God who moves through us.

Where Grace Met Me: Grace in the Smallest Places

It happened in the checkout line of a grocery store on a day that already felt too heavy to carry. I was juggling more than a few things, an overdrawn bank account, a weary body, and the silent shame of feeling like I couldn't keep up with life's demands. I had a cart full of essentials, just the basics: bread, milk, eggs, and a few frozen meals to get us through the week.

When I reached the register, I realized I didn't have my wallet.

The world didn't stop spinning, but it felt like it did. My hands trembled as I began the humiliating task of explaining myself to the cashier, apologizing for wasting her time, for holding up the line, for existing in that moment so visibly vulnerable.

I was already halfway through putting things back when the woman behind me gently touched my arm. She didn't say much—just smiled and handed her card to the cashier.

"It's okay," she said softly. "Someone did this for me once. Just pay it forward."

Just pay it forward.

That moment didn't just lighten my grocery bill; it shifted something in my spirit. I had been spiraling inward, convinced that I was invisible, that no one saw how hard I was trying. Her gesture, simple, quiet, unprovoked, was the physical embodiment of grace. She didn't know my story. She didn't need to. She just saw a need and met it. She offered dignity where I felt shame. She gave without demanding anything in return.

That moment became a ripple.

A few weeks later, I found myself in a similar line, this time behind a woman struggling to manage a crying toddler and swipe a worn EBT card that kept declining. I remembered the warmth I felt from the woman in line that day, and before I could talk myself out of it, I stepped forward. "I've got it," I said. My heart beat loudly in my ears, but I smiled. "It's been a rough day for all of us."

She cried. I cried. And I realized that grace multiplies when we let it move through us.

But grace in action doesn't always come wrapped in generosity at the grocery store. Sometimes, it shows up when you're holding your tongue during an argument you could absolutely win. Or when you choose to hug your child after a meltdown instead of scolding them. Or when you text someone you haven't heard from in months, not to lecture them for disappearing, but just to say, "I'm here if you need anything."

There was a moment with my own child that stands out. It was late, past bedtime, and I was exhausted in every sense of the word. My patience had thinned to nothing. He had refused to brush his teeth for the fifth night in a row, and I could feel the sharpness of my own voice rising. But something inside me paused. Grace whispered, *"Try again."* I crouched down, looked him in the eyes, and asked, "Hey... is something bothering you tonight?" He burst into tears. Turns out, he was scared about something he saw at school. He just didn't have the words.

That's the thing about grace; it makes room for the story behind the behavior.

Another time, grace showed up in a text message I didn't want to send. A friend and I had grown distant after a misunderstanding. I felt wronged, unseen, maybe even a little righteous in my silence. But one day, as I was praying, her name came to mind again. I sighed and sent a message: *"I've been thinking of you. No pressure, but I'm here if you ever want to talk."* She responded hours later, with a voice note filled with tears and thanks. She'd been waiting for a sign that it was safe to reconnect. Grace made that possible.

These aren't glamorous moments. No one clapped. There were no social media posts to commemorate them. But they were holy.

This is grace in action. It's inconvenient. It's vulnerable. And it's powerful.

Reflection & Spiritual Insight

Looking back, I've come to understand that grace is not a grand event; it is a spiritual reflex. It's the pause before the reaction. The softening of the heart when pride wants to stand tall. It is choosing love when judgment feels easier. Grace in action is not about being a hero; it's about being human, led by the Spirit, moment by moment.

In the story of the woman behind me at the grocery store, I encountered something far more profound than a paid grocery bill. I encountered a divine interruption. That interaction wasn't just between two women in a checkout line; it was God stepping into the ordinary and saying, *"I see you. I care for you. You are not alone."*

This is how God often moves, through us. We are His vessels, His hands and feet. And yet, we so often underestimate the power of small, faithful actions.

Scripture reminds us in Galatians 6:9, *"Let us not become weary in doing good, for at the proper time we will reap a harvest if we do not give up."* Grace in action is tiring sometimes. It asks more of us than we expect to give. But it also sows seeds of healing, community, and restoration.

When Jesus washed His disciples' feet in John 13, He wasn't just modeling humility; He was offering a blueprint. He said, *"I have set you an example that you should do as I have done for you"* (John 13:15). This wasn't symbolic; it was practical. Touching the dust of someone else's journey, wiping away their weariness, meeting them at their dirtiest and saying, "You are worthy of love", that is grace in motion.

I've learned that grace often means going first.

Grace is the first to say, *"I'm sorry."* The first to forgive. The first to ask, *"How are you, really?"* The first to let someone merge in traffic. The first to stop scrolling and say, *"I'm praying for you."*

These don't feel spiritual. But they are.

Jesus did not change the world through politics or power plays; He changed it through presence. Through meals shared, wounds touched, eyes met. He moved with grace, toward the outcast, the weary, the sinner, the doubter. And He calls us to do the same.

The more I practice grace in action, the more I realize it's not about being the fixer or the answer-bearer. It's about being available. Grace doesn't always solve the problem, but it always shifts the atmosphere.

Sometimes grace is letting someone go ahead in line. Sometimes grace is picking up the phone. Sometimes grace is staying quiet when you could be right.

And sometimes, grace is giving someone the benefit of the doubt,again.

These aren't easy things. But they are sacred.

In the parable of the Good Samaritan (Luke 10:25–37), Jesus redefines what it means to be a neighbor, not by proximity, but by compassion. The Samaritan didn't just feel bad for the wounded man. He stopped. He got off his donkey. He bandaged the wounds. He used his own money. He *stayed* in the discomfort. Grace doesn't just look. Grace acts.

I want to live like that. I want my life to tell the story of someone who didn't just understand grace but lived it, who chose to embody God's love even when it wasn't convenient, comfortable, or easy.

That's the invitation: not to be perfect, but to be willing. To be present. To be gracious.

And grace, when lived out loud, becomes a light. A map. A balm. A seed. A story someone else may one day tell.

Related Bible Stories or Characters

When I think of grace in action, I immediately think of the story Jesus told in Luke 10, the parable of **The Good Samaritan**. It's one of those Bible stories we hear so often that we risk skimming over it, but if we pause and look closely, it's a stunning blueprint for how grace works when it moves.

Here's the context: a man is traveling from Jerusalem to Jericho when he's attacked by robbers, stripped, beaten, and left for dead. Two religious leaders pass him by, first a priest, then a Levite. These were the people expected to help. The ones with the *titles*, the *platforms*, the *training*. But they kept walking.

Then comes the twist. A Samaritan, someone from a group despised by the Jews, sees the man and does the unthinkable. He stops. He feels compassion. He bandages the man's wounds, pours oil and wine on them, puts him on his donkey, brings him to an inn, and pays for his care.

This is grace in action.

The Samaritan had every reason to pass by. Cultural tension, inconvenience, cost, emotional risk. But grace doesn't ask, *"What do I owe?"* Grace asks, *"How can I love?"*

Jesus ends the story with a simple but profound question:

"Which of these three do you think was a neighbor to the man who fell into the hands of robbers?" The expert in the law replied, "The one who had mercy on him." Jesus told him, "Go and do likewise." (*Luke 10:36–37*)

Go and do likewise.

This story cuts through theology and lands directly in our Monday mornings and Tuesday afternoons. It's not about titles or proximity or beliefs; it's about action. Grace means stopping when the world says keep moving. Grace means seeing the wounds others ignore. Grace means saying, *"Your pain matters to me."*

Another example of grace in action is found in the story of **Boaz and Ruth**. Ruth was a foreigner, a widow, and a woman; three strikes in her cultural context. Yet Boaz, a man of power and privilege, noticed her. Not in a romanticized way, but in a protective, generous, God-honoring way. He told his workers to leave extra grain for her. He ensured she was safe while gleaning. He didn't just admire Ruth's loyalty to her mother-in-law, Naomi—he honored it with provision and kindness.

Grace doesn't always look like grand sacrifice. Sometimes it's leaving extra room. Making space. Sharing what you have. Boaz could've ignored Ruth, as most would have. But grace notices the ones the world overlooks.

And, of course, no conversation about grace in action is complete without pointing to **Jesus Himself**. Every moment of His ministry was grace in motion. He healed the unclean, ate with the outcast, spoke gently to the brokenhearted, and stood up for those who had no voice. In Matthew 25:40, He makes it clear that whatever we do for *the least of these*, we do for Him. Every cup of water. Every open door. Every second chance.

Grace, at its core, is about how we treat each other.

Gray Space Exploration

Grace in action doesn't always feel clean or certain. In fact, it often lives in the *gray*, that murky space where boundaries blur, where love and exhaustion meet, where we're not sure what's "right," only what feels *real*.

There's a certain comfort in binary thinking, black and white, yes or no, right or wrong. But life rarely fits into such tidy categories.

One of the hardest parts of embodying grace is choosing to act when the situation doesn't come with a script.

What do you do when someone hurts you repeatedly, and you're exhausted from forgiving? What do you do when your coworker slacks off, but you know they're struggling behind the scenes? What does grace look like when you're setting boundaries, with someone you still love?

Here's the thing: grace in action doesn't mean ignoring pain or pretending everything is okay. It doesn't mean being a doormat or avoiding truth. Sometimes, the most gracious thing you can do is to speak up, with kindness. Sometimes, grace is stepping back instead of stepping in. Other times, grace is staying, even when you'd rather run.

One of the trickiest gray areas I've navigated is learning when to help and when to hold back. There were times I wanted to jump in and "fix" everything for someone I loved, but grace reminded me that people also need the dignity of their own process. I had to learn that grace is not controlling. It doesn't smother. It trusts God to do the deeper work.

Another messy gray space? Choosing grace when I didn't feel like it—when I was tired, offended, or when someone *didn't deserve it.* That phrase, "deserve", is slippery. Because if we're honest, none of us deserve the grace God gives so freely. That's the whole point. It's unearned. Unmerited. Lavish. And we're called to pour it out anyway, especially when it costs us.

Grace doesn't require that we be perfect; it invites us to stay tender in an imperfect world.

It's messy. It's nuanced. But that's exactly where grace *lives*, not in the certainty of rules, but in the holy tension of love, humility, discernment, and sacrifice.

Connection to the Reader's Life

Let's be honest: grace in action sounds beautiful on paper, but in real life? It's *hard*.

It's hard to be the one who forgives *again* when the hurt is still tender. It's hard to send that "just checking in" text to someone who never replied to the last one. It's hard to be kind when you're exhausted, to be gentle when you feel unseen, to serve when no one says thank you.

And yet, you keep showing up.

If you're reading this, you've probably extended grace more times than you can count. You've bitten your tongue when your pride wanted to speak. You've given the benefit of the doubt when suspicion whispered louder. You've walked into rooms where you weren't sure your kindness would be returned. That is not weakness. That is strength. That is grace in motion.

Maybe there's someone in your life right now who drains you, frustrates you, or simply doesn't reciprocate what you offer. Maybe you're holding a grudge you don't know how to let go of. Maybe you're waiting for someone else to take the first step, say the first word, make the first move.

What if grace goes first?

What if grace sends the text, starts the conversation, writes the apology, offers the ride, shares the meal, opens the door?

Grace doesn't mean pretending everything is fine. It doesn't mean tolerating abuse or abandoning your own needs. But it *does* mean choosing love over vengeance. Compassion over convenience. Patience over pride.

And here's the good news: grace is not about you getting it right every time. It's about returning to love when you'd rather retreat into silence.It's about being willing to try again, to soften when you want to harden. It's about seeing your daily actions, yes, even the smallest ones, as sacred opportunities to be the hands and feet of Jesus.

So here's my question for you: Where is grace asking you to move?

Maybe it's toward someone you've written off. Maybe it's in how you respond to your kids when they push every button. Maybe it's in how you speak to yourself when you mess up.

Start small. One step. One word. One act.

Grace is not about the size of the gesture; it's about the posture of your heart.

You don't have to change the world today. But you *can* change someone's moment. And sometimes, that's exactly where the kingdom begins.

Practical Application / Tools for Grace

Grace is not a passive feeling; it's a muscle. And like any muscle, it gets stronger with use. Below are simple, intentional ways to begin practicing grace in action in your daily life. You don't need a platform, a pulpit, or a perfect personality. You just need willingness, and a heart that stays open.

1. The "Go First" Challenge

Once this week, choose to be the one who initiates grace.

- Send the first text.

- Offer the first smile.

- Say "I'm sorry" first, even if your pride flinches. Sometimes, going first is the most powerful act of grace you'll ever make.

2. The Five-Minute Favor

Set aside five minutes a day to do something purely for someone else's benefit.

- Write a note of encouragement.

- Drop off coffee for a coworker.

- Offer to help carry groceries or open a door. Let grace become a rhythm in your everyday tasks.

3. Prayer Before Reaction

Before responding in frustration, pause. Breathe. Whisper a simple prayer:

"Lord, help me see them through Your eyes. Let my response reflect Your grace, not my anger." Even a one-second pause can change everything.

4. Keep a Grace Journal

At the end of each day, write down:

- One moment someone extended grace to you

- One moment you extended grace to someone else This small practice builds awareness and gratitude for grace in motion.

5. Weekly Grace Practice

Choose one specific act of grace to practice each week:

- Forgive someone (even silently)

- Compliment someone you usually criticize

- Leave a kind note for a stranger

- Let someone go ahead of you in line Watch how these small actions ripple outward.

6. Memorize a "Grace Verse"

Choose a scripture that anchors your heart in grace. Write it on a sticky note and place it where you'll see it often. A few favorites:

- *"Be kind and compassionate to one another, forgiving each other, just as in Christ God forgave you."* – Ephesians 4:32

- *"Whatever you did for the least of these... you did for me."* – Matthew 25:40

- *"Let your conversation be always full of grace, seasoned with salt."* – Colossians 4:6

7. Create a "Grace Toolkit" for Hard Days

When you're running on empty, it's harder to give grace. Build a go-to list of quick practices:

- Step outside and breathe deeply

- Text a friend to pray for you

- Repeat a breath prayer: Inhale: *"I choose grace..."* Exhale: *"...even here."*

Grace doesn't ask you to be perfect. It just invites you to be present.

Reflection Questions

These questions are meant to meet you where you are. Whether you're reading this in the quiet of early morning or in the middle of a chaotic day, take a moment to pause, reflect, and invite God to speak to your heart through these prompts.

1. **When was the last time someone extended grace to you in a tangible way? How did it make you feel?**

2. **Who in your life is most difficult to show grace to right now? What would it look like to act in grace toward them, even in a small way?**

3. **What stops you from offering grace in daily moments, pride, fear, exhaustion, the need to be right?**

4. **What are some small ways you can begin practicing grace in your current season of life?**

5. **How does your understanding of grace change when you imagine it as movement, something alive, active, and ongoing?**

Use these questions for journaling, small group discussion, or quiet prayer. Let them stretch your heart, not to shame you, but to awaken something deeper.

Closing Blessing

May you be the kind of person who chooses grace even when it's hard. May your hands move in love, your voice speak with kindness, and your presence reflect the gentle strength of Christ.

When the world feels cold, may you be warmth. When people are difficult, may you be patient. When grace feels undeserved, may you remember how freely it was given to you.

Let your everyday moments become sacred ones. Let your ordinary actions be drenched in holy purpose. And when you grow weary, may you hear the whisper of heaven:

"You're doing better than you think. Keep going. Keep loving. Keep choosing grace."

Amen.

Chapter Seven

♥

"You then, my child, be strong in the grace that is in Christ Jesus."

2 Timothy 2:1 (NRSV)

Setting the Tone

Sometimes grace doesn't shout. It doesn't announce itself with lightning bolts or grand gestures. Sometimes, it whispers through generations, echoing in the quiet ways we choose to show up for each other. It's not always in the dramatic acts of forgiveness or miraculous moments of healing. Often, grace is a phone call returned, a birthday remembered, a child protected, a wound tended with care rather than retaliation. The legacy of grace is not just the story we tell; it's the story we leave behind. It's how we show others the way to keep loving, even when it's hard.

Chapter Summary

In this chapter, we explore the quiet, enduring strength of grace that outlives the moment and echoes into the lives of those who follow. The legacy of grace is not measured in accolades or public praise but in the steady, compassionate choices made over time. It's found in how we treat those who hurt us, how we raise the next generation, and how we show up with empathy even when we have every reason to withhold it.

We will examine how grace leaves a spiritual and emotional inheritance, shaping not only who we are but who we become, and who we allow others to become. This chapter acknowledges the tension between hurt and healing, between the past we inherited and the future we hope to create. It asks: what kind of grace will you pass down?

Where Grace Met Me: Love Without a Script

I never set out to create a legacy. Most of us don't. We're just trying to survive the moment, get through the season, make the next right decision. Legacy feels like something distant, something reserved for grandparents and historical figures. But somewhere along the way, between scraped knees and sleepless nights, between silent prayers and whispered apologies, I started to realize that legacy isn't something we plan for later. It's something we build right now, moment by moment, choice by choice.

I was reminded of this one ordinary Tuesday morning. The kind of morning that feels uneventful on the surface, cereal bowls still sitting in the sink, a half-folded pile of laundry on the couch, a toddler clinging to my leg while I tried to answer emails. I had just gotten off the phone with my mother, who'd called to confirm the details for an upcoming trip we were all taking as a family. My mother. My father. My husband. Our children. Together.

If someone had told my childhood self that one day my divorced parents, who had once stood in different corners of a room like strangers holding invisible swords, would travel together with their grandchildren, I wouldn't have believed it. I would've laughed. Or cried. Or both. Because for so long, peace between them seemed impossible. The silence between their sentences used to carry more weight than the words themselves.

But something changed.

And that change didn't come in a single dramatic apology or overnight miracle. It came in the long, slow work of grace.

I still remember the early years after the divorce. I was young, old enough to feel the tension but not old enough to understand it. My father moved out swiftly, and everything about our lives shifted in an instant. We were suddenly caught in this odd choreography, weekends with dad, weekdays with mom. Birthday parties split down the middle. School events negotiated like treaties. There was a time when I felt like the rope in an invisible tug-of-war, and all I wanted was for someone to drop the rope.

But even in those early years, I caught glimmers of grace. I didn't have the language for it then, but I see it clearly now.

Like the time my father drove two hours just to attend my eighth-grade spelling bee. He didn't stay long, just long enough to smile, hug me, and whisper, "I'm proud of you." He was back on the road before the applause had stopped. At the time, I thought nothing of it. Now, I see the quiet grace of presence. He showed up.

Or the way my mother, who had every right to be bitter, still ironed my church dress the night before I went to visit my father. She didn't speak ill of him in front of me. She didn't roll her eyes when I mentioned his name. That, too, was grace. The kind that chooses peace over pride.

Over the years, I watched my parents soften. They didn't reconcile romantically, but they reconciled relationally. They made peace with the past and prioritized the future. For them, grace looked like compromise. Like learning how to sit beside someone who once broke your heart, not out of obligation, but out of love for the child you created together.

I remember one Thanksgiving vividly. I had recently graduated from graduate school and was hosting my first big holiday dinner. The nerves were real, I wanted the food to be perfect, the table to be Instagram-worthy, the energy to be light. But looming above all that was one major question: Would my parents be able to be in the same room without reigniting old wounds?

I shouldn't have worried.

They arrived separately, of course. But when my dad walked in and saw my mom, he smiled and said, "Wow, you look just like you did when we met." I held my breath. My mom laughed, really laughed, and replied, "So do you, plus a few pounds."

We all exhaled.

That dinner was more than a meal. It was a moment. A holy one. Not because everything was perfect, but because grace sat at the head of the table. The same grace that had walked us through courtrooms and custody schedules now offered us sweet potato pie and second chances. That night, I saw something I had prayed for but never expected: restoration without resentment.

That legacy, the one I thought I didn't have, is now what I'm most proud to pass on. My children see it in ways they may not yet understand. They see grandparents who share hugs, not hostility. They see their mama loving both her parents with no shame and no side-taking. They see that family doesn't have to be picture-perfect to be whole.

And perhaps most importantly, they're learning that forgiveness is not weakness. It's strength wrapped in softness. It's the quiet courage to keep choosing love, again and again, even when it would be easier not to.

Grace does that.

It builds bridges where there were once burned-down barns. It holds space for sorrow without letting it swallow joy. It allows us to rewrite the story, not to erase the hard chapters, but to give them a redemptive ending.

Now, when I think about legacy, I don't think about wealth or fame or perfectly framed family photos. I think about the small, sacred ways we choose grace every day. I think about my parents showing up, together, for school plays and baby dedications. I think about my sister and me, once divided by childhood pain, now united in adulthood by healing. I think about the way my children run into their grandparents' arms, unaware of the long journey that made such a moment possible.

That's the legacy of grace.

It doesn't always roar. Sometimes, it simply whispers: "Keep going. Keep forgiving. Keep loving. The next generation is watching."

Reflection & Spiritual Insight

As I reflect on the quiet miracles that make up my family's story, I realize that grace often works in subtle ways. It doesn't always look like transformation in real time. Sometimes, it moves through years of silence, awkward conversations, and quiet endurance before it shows its fruit. Grace works like water on stone; it doesn't rush; it reshapes.

The legacy my parents passed down wasn't perfect. But it was powerful. It showed me that broken relationships don't have to stay broken. That what starts in separation can grow into cooperation. That bitterness doesn't have to be inherited. I saw two people choose peace over pride, again and again. And that steady choosing, that holy repetition, that was the grace.

What strikes me most now is that legacy is formed in moments that often feel too small to matter. A decision not to lash out. A ride offered. A text sent instead of ignored. Legacy lives in the love we show when it's not required, in the bridges we build when no one's watching.

In 2 Timothy 2:1, Paul writes, "Be strong in the grace that is in Christ Jesus." That verse doesn't just urge us to receive grace; it calls us to carry it. To live it out with strength. It's not a passive, gentle suggestion. It's a call to spiritual resilience. To hold onto grace when resentment tempts you. To walk in grace when you feel tired, offended, or forgotten.

Grace is not weakness. It is strength cloaked in softness. It is power under restraint. And when we live that kind of grace, it leaves finger-prints on the hearts of everyone who crosses our path, especially our children, our partners, our community.

We may never know how much healing our grace sparked in someone else's life. But we don't need to. Our job is simply to sow it. To plant the seeds of grace, trusting that God will water them in ways we cannot see.

My parents didn't get everything right. But they got one thing right: they chose grace even when it wasn't easy. That choice changed the trajectory of our entire family. That's the legacy I want to leave behind, not perfection, not polished faith, but resilient, relational grace that holds people together when life wants to tear them apart.

Related Bible Story: Ruth and Naomi

When I think of a biblical legacy built through grace, I think of Naomi and Ruth. Their story in the book of Ruth isn't just about loyalty; it's about grace passed down in real time, through pain, through loss, and through uncertain futures.

Naomi had every reason to turn inward. She had lost her husband, her sons, her home. She renamed herself "Mara," which means bitter. And yet, even in her grief, she didn't push Ruth away. She allowed Ruth to stay. She allowed herself to be accompanied. That alone is grace, to not isolate in the storm, but to receive love even when you feel emptied out.

And Ruth, oh, Ruth. Her decision to stay, to speak those iconic words, "Where you go, I will go. Your people will be my people. Your God, my God", was not just about love. It was about planting a new legacy. She chose to tie her life to a woman who had nothing to offer her but faith and shared grief. That's grace in its purest form: commitment without condition.

What followed was a series of redemptive moments, moments that led Ruth to Boaz, and ultimately to becoming the great-grandmother of King David, and part of the lineage of Jesus Christ. That's the ripple effect of grace. A widow's weary love became a legacy that reached into eternity.

Naomi's story reminds us that even when we feel like we've lost everything, grace can still be born. Ruth's story reminds us that grace is sometimes choosing to stay when leaving would be easier. And together, their story reminds us that legacy is not defined by what you leave behind; it's defined by how you walk with people through the hard parts.

We all carry the potential to pass down either bitterness or grace. Our actions echo into generations we may never meet. May we, like Ruth and Naomi, choose grace, and trust God to build a legacy beyond what we can imagine.

Gray Space Exploration

Legacy is rarely clean. It's not a curated photo album or a single, defining moment; it's a blur of choices, a mess of contradictions, a series of tensions held together by love and effort. That's what makes it sacred. And that's what makes it gray.

When I look at the story of my parents, I don't see a fairy tale. I see confusion, heartbreak, silence, tension... and grace. I see two people who hurt each other deeply, and then chose, slowly and imperfectly, to show up anyway. That's not black and white. That's not good versus bad. That's human.

The gray space in legacy is this: sometimes the very people who wound us also teach us how to heal. Sometimes the ones who broke our hearts become the ones who show us how to keep loving. It's messy. It's uncomfortable. It's the paradox of grace, that it often comes through the same door as pain.

We live in a culture that prefers clean stories. We want heroes and villains. We want resolution. We want to be able to say, "This person was right, and this person was wrong." But life doesn't work like that. Relationships don't work like that. Families don't work like that.

What do you do when someone's presence has been both harmful and healing? When a parent disappointed you in ways that shaped you... but also showed up in ways that saved you?

You live in the gray.

You hold space for both truths.

You stop waiting for the story to make perfect sense, and instead, you let grace be the thread that holds the contradictions together.

Grace doesn't ask you to pretend the hurt never happened. It asks you not to let it have the final word.

In my own life, I've had to learn how to stop waiting for the perfect apology or the clean ending. I've had to release the version of my parents I hoped they'd be and embrace the beautifully flawed people they actually are. I've had to sit in the tension of gratitude and grief, thankful for what I had, and grieving what I didn't.

That's the gray.

And in that space, I've seen God move the most. Not in the absolutes. Not in the extremes. But right in the middle of the mess, offering healing, offering redemption, offering legacy through the unexpected vehicle of grace.

Connection to Reader's Life

Maybe your story looks different. Maybe your parents never found their way back to peace. Maybe you're the one trying to hold a fractured family together with nothing but hope and tired hands. Or maybe you're building your legacy from scratch, with no blueprint, no gentle examples, and no elders to show you how.

Here's what I want you to know: the legacy of grace is not about having a perfect past. It's about making powerful choices in the present. Right now, you are shaping what will ripple forward into the lives of those around you. Every time you choose kindness when you could choose distance, every time you say "I forgive you" when your pride screams "you owe me," every time you show up, even with shaking hands, that's grace. And it matters.

Legacy isn't reserved for those with grandchildren and generational wealth. It's for anyone willing to love on purpose. Anyone who is brave enough to choose empathy over resentment. Anyone who breaks a cycle instead of repeating it.

Maybe you're the first in your family to even *talk* about grace. Maybe you're the first to apologize. The first to set a boundary. The first to say, "I love you" without strings attached. That, too, is legacy.

And maybe you're wondering, what if I don't have children? What if I'm still in the middle of the mess? What if no one sees the work I'm doing?

Friend, your legacy isn't measured by visibility. It's measured by impact. And impact often begins in hidden places, in how you speak to yourself when you fail, in how you respond to the person who hurt you, in how you reflect Christ in rooms where no one knows His name.

That's grace in motion. That's legacy in bloom.

Think about the people who have shaped you. Not the ones with power or platforms, but the ones who made you feel seen. The teacher who stayed after class to encourage you. The grandparent who listened without judgment. The friend who forgave you when you didn't deserve it. What they gave you wasn't just a kind moment; it was inheritance. They planted grace into your life. And now, it lives in you.

So ask yourself: What do I want to leave behind? What kind of spiritual, emotional, relational legacy am I writing with my life? And how can I begin, even today, to let grace be my legacy?

You don't have to have it all figured out. You don't have to get it right every time. But if you can start with one act of grace, toward yourself, toward someone else, you are already shaping something eternal.

Grace doesn't erase the past. It transforms the future.

And you, right now, wherever you are, have the power to carry that future forward.

Practical Application / Tools for Grace

Legacy is built not in one grand moment but in thousands of quiet ones. These practices are designed to help you cultivate a lifestyle of grace, one that outlives you, blesses others, and reflects the heart of God in everyday life.

1. Legacy Letters Write a letter to someone who has shaped you with their grace, whether they're still living or not. Express what their kindness, forgiveness, or presence meant to you. You don't even have to send it. Just writing it is a way to honor their legacy and recognize how grace travels from heart to heart.

You can also write a letter to someone you hope to influence, your child, your younger self, a future version of you. What do you want them to know about grace? What would you hope they learn from your life?

2. The Grace Ripple Journal For 7 days, journal about one act of grace you gave or received each day. It can be big or small, a conversation you navigated with patience, a moment you forgave yourself for a mistake, or a stranger's unexpected kindness. At the end of the week, reflect on what patterns you see and how grace is already flowing through your life.

Prompt:

Where did grace show up today? How did it impact me, or someone else?

3. Family Grace Rituals Create a new ritual that reinforces grace as a value in your home or relationships. This could be as simple as:

- A "grace moment" during dinner where each person shares one thing they're grateful for or one place they saw kindness that day.

- A monthly forgiveness prayer where you release grudges or regrets.

- Celebrating growth, not just achievements, by affirming someone's effort, heart, or healing.

Small traditions like these build emotional and spiritual inheritance.

4. Practice "First Grace" Responses Train yourself to respond with grace, first and foremost. The next time someone disappoints you, pauses awkwardly, or triggers an old wound, try this silent breath prayer before reacting:

Inhale: "God, let me lead with grace..." Exhale: "...not ego, not fear, not pain."

Then choose your next action deliberately. Respond, don't react.

5. Start a Grace Legacy Jar Find a jar or box and some small slips of paper. Over time, add:

- Moments when you witnessed or offered grace

- Quotes or verses that inspire you

- Names of people who have modeled grace in your life

- Prayers for future generations

Review your jar at the end of each season to see how your legacy is taking shape in real time.

Grace builds slowly. But with intention, it becomes the most powerful inheritance you could ever offer.

Reflection Questions

1. When you think about the legacy you've inherited, emotionally, spiritually, relationally, what has been beautiful? What has been painful? How has grace helped you hold both?

2. Who in your life has modeled grace for you? How did their actions shape the way you think about forgiveness, love, or compassion?

3. What small acts of grace do you want to become known for? What do you hope others feel when they experience your presence?

4. Where are you being invited to plant seeds of grace that may not bloom in your lifetime, but still matter?

5. If future generations could read a single paragraph about how you lived with grace, what would you hope it would say?

Closing Blessing & Prayer

Blessing May your life whisper grace long after your voice has quieted. May the way you forgive, show up, and love without condition become a healing inheritance for those who come after you. May your presence plant seeds of peace where bitterness once grew. May your legacy not be one of perfection, but of compassion, courage, and kindness. And may you always remember that what you build in grace will never be forgotten in eternity.

Prayer God of mercy and memory, Thank You for the unseen ways grace is shaping our stories. Help us to live not just for ourselves but for the ones watching us, the children, the neighbors, the strangers, the future. Let our words reflect Your love. Let our actions echo Your gentleness. Teach us to forgive with open hands and to lead with open hearts. When we are tempted to withhold grace, remind us of how freely You give it. Let us be vessels of healing, even when we are still healing ourselves. And may the legacy we leave behind be rooted in Your truth, marked by Your mercy, and blooming with grace that multiplies for generations to come. Amen.

Chapter Eight

♥

"I am about to do a new thing; now it springs forth, do you not perceive it? I will make a way in the wilderness and rivers in the desert."

Isaiah 43:19 (NRSV)

Change doesn't ask for permission. It doesn't wait for your calendar to clear or for your heart to feel ready. It knocks quietly at first, then kicks the door wide open. And in the whirlwind, as life rearranges itself and the things you once depended on fall away or shift beneath your feet, it can be easy to forget that grace walks in with change, hand in hand. Grace may not make the transition feel easier at first. But if you pause, just for a moment, you might catch a glimpse of her. Whispering comfort in the chaos. Offering strength when you feel undone. Reminding you that you are not alone in the becoming.

Chapter Summary

This chapter is about the kind of grace that sustains us when life demands we evolve. It is for the woman who is letting go of a version of herself she once clung to. For the father stepping into a role he never expected. For the student, the dreamer, the believer, standing at the edge of something new, afraid to leap but unable to stay where they are.

Change, whether invited or imposed, stretches us. It dismantles the familiar and exposes our longing for certainty. Yet within that discomfort, grace flows like water, gentle and persistent. Grace does not promise us control. Instead, it invites us to trust. To release our white-knuckled grip on what was and open our hands to what could be. When everything shifts, grace becomes the steady ground beneath our feet.

Where Grace Met Me: The Beauty of Becoming

The first morning I brought my newborn son home, I stood in the doorway of his nursery holding him with trembling arms, not from weakness, but from the quiet weight of awe, and fear.

The walls were painted a soft hue of lavender, the crib freshly assembled with elephant sheets I had obsessively picked out two months before. A mobile spun lazily overhead, clouds and stars turning in time with the soft hum of a lullaby I had played on loop while folding onesies and imagining what his cry might sound like. I had longed for this room. Prayed for this child. Dreamed of this moment. And yet... I felt unprepared.

I had spent years believing I would never be a mother. Diagnoses, medical procedures, failed attempts, and the cruel silence of waiting had taught me to protect my hope by keeping it small. Even after the first miraculous pregnancy, which ended in a devastating miscarriage, I had trained my heart not to get too attached. When this second pregnancy took root, I treaded lightly. I smiled, but cautiously. I bought tiny socks, but didn't remove the tags. Joy was shadowed by anxiety. Each ultrasound offered reassurance, but my soul remained guarded. I had learned how to brace for disappointment. I had not learned how to fully receive the miracle.

So here I was, baby boy in arms, heart thudding against my ribs like a prayer I hadn't fully spoken. His eyes fluttered open, then closed again. His breath, soft and rhythmic, sounded like the beginning of a new song. And suddenly, the tears came. Not just because I was tired, or hormonal, or overwhelmed. But because I knew that my life, my identity, my rhythms, my priorities, had been permanently rearranged.

There was no going back to who I was before him. I had entered a holy transition, and no one had warned me that grace would feel so tender and terrifying all at once.

Motherhood was not the perfectly curated version I had seen on Pinterest. It was night feedings with cracked nipples and bleary eyes. It was crying in the shower because I didn't know what I was doing, because I missed the freedom of my old life, and because I felt guilty for missing it at all. It was learning to love a body that didn't look or feel like mine anymore. It was arguing with my husband over who was more exhausted, more unseen, more stretched. It was reaching the end of myself daily, and finding, to my surprise, that God was already waiting there.

I remember one afternoon, maybe three months in, when I reached my breaking point. My son wouldn't stop crying. I had tried everything, feeding, burping, rocking, swaddling, singing the same lullaby until my throat was dry. Nothing worked. I placed him in his crib, walked into the bathroom, and slid down the wall, sobbing with my face in my hands. I felt like a failure. Like I had prayed for a blessing and then ruined it with my inadequacy.

But right there, on the cool tile floor, grace found me.

Not in the form of an answer, but in a moment of surrender. A whisper from somewhere deep inside: *You don't have to do this perfectly. You just have to show up.* And I had shown up. Every day. Every hour. Every exhausted, uncertain moment. That was enough. That was grace.

It wasn't long after that moment that a friend dropped off dinner with a sticky note that said, "You're doing better than you think." I kept that note for months. On days I couldn't feel God's presence, that note reminded me He was still speaking, through meals, through mercy, through the kindness of a friend who knew that change doesn't require perfection, only presence.

Motherhood changed everything, but not all at once. Some parts of me were stripped away, yes. But other parts were uncovered, revealed, born anew. In learning to care for a child, I was also learning to care for myself. In surrendering control, I found strength I didn't know I had. And in the places where I felt the weakest, grace whispered, *You are still becoming. Let that be enough.*

Change rarely looks the way we imagined. It's not always wrapped in beauty or clarity. Sometimes it's a mess of tears, spit-up, and silence. But it is still sacred. And grace? Grace meets us right there, in the transformation, in the threshold, in the blurry middle of who we were and who we're becoming.

Reflection & Spiritual Insight

Change has a way of exposing us. It strips away the familiar and unearths every hidden insecurity, every buried fear, every illusion of control we once depended on. And yet, somehow, that exposure becomes sacred ground. Not because the process is easy or beautiful, but because God is present in it.

I didn't realize it at the time, but in those early months of motherhood, I was being re-formed. Not just into a parent, but into a woman who could trust without seeing. Who could surrender her expectations and still believe that God was holding every piece. I was learning to parent through grace, to live through grace, to let grace fill in the gaps between who I thought I should be and who I actually was.

One of the greatest lies we're tempted to believe in seasons of change is that we are alone. That everyone else has it figured out. That something must be wrong with us if we're struggling. But the truth is this: *struggle doesn't mean you're failing; it means you're human.* And grace was never meant for the perfect; it was always designed for the fragile, the tired, the ones who show up anyway.

Isaiah 43:19 says, *"See, I am doing a new thing! Now it springs up; do you not perceive it?"* This verse often gets quoted as a rally cry for new beginnings, but it is so much deeper than that. It's not just about embracing the "new thing." It's about learning to perceive it even when it's not obvious. It's about trusting that God is working, even when all we see is wilderness and wasteland. It's about recognizing that grace is not only at the finish line; it's in the wandering. In the breaking. In the messy in-between.

God was not asking me to master motherhood in a week. He was not demanding that I embrace change with a smile or suppress my anxiety with forced gratitude. He was inviting me to walk with Him, slowly, imperfectly, vulnerably, through the unknown. He was asking me to let go of who I thought I needed to be, and to receive the grace of simply becoming.

Looking back now, I see that grace came in layers. It was the resilience I didn't know I had. The friend who didn't judge my messy house or unwashed hair. The unexpected nap that saved my sanity. The Scripture that echoed in my spirit when I thought I had nothing left. Grace was not always loud, but it was always there.

Theology teaches us that grace is unmerited favor. But lived experience teaches us that grace is also *uninterrupted presence*. God doesn't step back when we're overwhelmed; He draws closer. Not to fix, but to hold. Not to erase the discomfort, but to remind us that we are not alone in it.

Change asks a lot of us. But grace gives more.

Grace doesn't eliminate the growing pains, but it transforms how we endure them. It reminds us that transformation isn't about perfection; it's about *presence*. God's presence. Our presence. The willingness to keep showing up to life, even when it looks nothing like what we expected.

If you're in a season of transition, grieving a loss, starting over, becoming someone new, know this: you're not failing. You're unfolding. And every step forward, no matter how shaky, is soaked in grace.

Related Bible Stories or Characters

One of the most powerful stories of grace in the midst of change is found in the life of **Ruth**. Her story is a quiet revolution, a testimony to what happens when life shifts unexpectedly, when the path you imagined disappears, and yet... you choose to keep walking.

Ruth's life was marked by a series of profound and painful transitions. A Moabite woman who had married into an Israelite family, she experienced a change most of us never feel ready for: the loss of her husband. Alongside her mother-in-law Naomi, who was also grieving the death of her own husband and sons, Ruth found herself in unfamiliar territory, emotionally and literally. Widowhood. Relocation. A new culture. A new people. A new faith.

Change wasn't a chapter in Ruth's story. It was the entire book.

And yet, embedded in Ruth's response to this upheaval is one of the clearest pictures of grace we have in Scripture, not just the grace she received, but the grace she extended. When Naomi urged her to return to her homeland and start over, Ruth replied with radical devotion: *"Where you go, I will go. Where you stay, I will stay. Your people will be my people, and your God my God"* (Ruth 1:16). It was a declaration not only of loyalty but of faith. Ruth chose to walk forward, not with answers, but with trust.

And it was in that movement, in that messy, uncertain transition, that grace began to unfold.

God's hand moved through every detail. The barley fields where Ruth gleaned just enough to survive. The moment Boaz noticed her. The unfolding of a love story built not on convenience, but on mutual respect and divine timing. Ruth went from being a foreign widow to the great-grandmother of King David, a lineage that would ultimately lead to Christ.

What does Ruth's story teach us about grace in transition?

It teaches us that grace meets us when we show up, even with nothing but broken pieces and brave hearts. That sometimes grace looks like *gleaning*, taking just enough for today, trusting there will be more tomorrow. That even when life as we knew it ends, a new beginning is still possible. That change, however painful, can birth legacy.

Ruth didn't rush the process. She didn't manipulate her circumstances or pretend to be okay. She just kept moving. Kept trusting. Kept choosing kindness. And God met her in it all, not with lightning bolts or booming declarations, but with open doors and divine alignments she couldn't have orchestrated herself.

Just like Ruth, we are invited to walk through change not with certainty, but with grace. Her story reminds us that every detour can be sacred, and every ending might just be the beginning of something redemptive.

Gray Space Exploration

Change is rarely clear-cut.

There's the excitement of something new... and the grief of what you had to leave behind. There's the hope for what's ahead... tangled up with the fear that you won't be enough to meet it. There's the joy of a baby's first giggle... coupled with the loneliness of not recognizing yourself in the mirror anymore.

This is the gray space, where contradictions coexist.

For me, stepping into motherhood wasn't just a transition. It was a complete dismantling of my former self. The version of me who could sleep eight hours, who had time to linger in the quiet, who could finish a thought, or a sentence, without being interrupted by cries or bottles or appointments.

She didn't disappear, but she was deeply rearranged.

And the hardest part? I missed her.

I missed who I used to be. I missed the simplicity, the independence, the illusion of control. But I also loved my child fiercely. I loved this new chapter. And it was confusing to hold both emotions at once, to be overflowing with gratitude and yet aching with the loss of familiarity.

This is the part no one tells you about. The part that's hard to say out loud. Because we live in a culture that wants clear narratives. "You should be so happy." "You're so blessed."And yes, both are true. But it is also true that blessings can stretch you. That even miracles come with mourning. That change, even good change, can feel like grief.

There was no villain in my story. No one to blame. Nothing necessarily went "wrong." And yet, there was tension. Emotional fatigue. Silent tears. Identity crisis. A sense of being both too much and not enough, all at once.

Grace lived in that complexity.

It wasn't trying to fix me or rush me. Grace didn't show up with answers; it showed up with *permission*. Permission to feel both joy and loss. Permission to grow slowly. Permission to not have it all together.

The gray space of change is where we learn to hold paradox without shame. It's where we learn that uncertainty is not failure; it's part of the process. It's where we learn to stop asking, "Am I doing this right?" and start asking, "Can I let God meet me here, in the mess of it all?"

Because the truth is, some of the most sacred moments in life happen in the blur, not when everything is sorted out, but when we decide to keep walking through the fog, believing grace will meet us with every step.

Connection to Reader's Life

Dear reader, can I ask you something tender?

What are you carrying right now that no one else sees?

Is it the quiet ache of a life you didn't expect? A relationship that shifted so gradually you barely noticed the distance until it felt like silence? A job you once prayed for that now feels heavy? A version of yourself you thought you'd be by now, but aren't?

Maybe you're navigating a change you chose, a new city, a new baby, a new chapter, and still, it feels like you're drowning some days. Or maybe change chose *you*. A diagnosis. A goodbye. A door closed that you weren't ready to walk away from. Maybe you're in the middle of something blurry, undefined, between who you used to be and who you're not quite yet.

And here's the truth that most people won't say out loud: change is beautiful and brutal all at once. You're allowed to grieve what you lost, even while being grateful for what's coming. You're allowed to be tired from growing. You're allowed to feel overwhelmed, even when you know God is in it.

You're allowed to need grace.

Because change, no matter how small or seismic, will ask more of you than you think you can give. It will stretch your faith, rearrange your identity, and confront you with parts of yourself you didn't know were fragile. And yet, it will also reveal new strength, new softness, and a deeper capacity for love, trust, and presence.

You don't need to have it all figured out. You don't need a five-step plan. What you need, more than perfection, more than certainty, is to believe that grace is big enough to hold you through it. Through the awkward middle. Through the fatigue. Through the fear. Through the slow becoming.

So let me ask gently:

Where is change happening in your life right now? What are you afraid to admit about how hard it's been? What part of yourself are you mourning, even if no one else understands? Where do you most need grace to meet you?

Take a breath. Release the pressure. Let this be your reminder: You are not behind. You are not broken. You are simply becoming. And that? That is holy work.

You are being held, right here, right now, in the beautiful, blurry middle of it all.

Practical Application / Tools for Grace in Change

Grace isn't just a feeling; it's a *practice*. Especially in seasons of transition, when everything feels uncertain and shaky, we need anchors, small, sacred rhythms that remind us we're not lost. That God is still present. That we are still whole, even when life feels in pieces.

Here are tools to help you walk through change with gentleness, faith, and grace:

1. The "Noticing" Practice

Each morning, ask yourself:

- *What is changing in me?*

- *What feels hard today?*

- *Where can I notice grace, even if it's small?*

Keep a notebook by your bed or phone notes app open. This isn't about solving anything; it's about creating space to witness your own becoming.

2. Grace-Based Affirmations

Speak these aloud when fear or doubt rises:

- "I don't need to have it all together to be worthy of grace."

- "Change is uncomfortable, but not unsafe; God is here."

- "I am still growing, and that is enough."

- "Becoming takes time, and I give myself permission to unfold slowly."

Write them on sticky notes. Leave them on mirrors, dashboards, laptops, wherever you tend to forget you're still held.

3. The "Release and Receive" Breath Prayer

Inhale deeply: *"God, I release what no longer serves me..."* Exhale slowly: *"...and I receive the grace to become who You're calling me to be."*

Repeat this whenever you feel overwhelmed. Let your breath become your prayer.

4. Anchor People, Anchor Places

List 2–3 people or places that help you feel grounded when life is swirling. Maybe it's a trusted friend, a parent, your pastor, a park bench, or your favorite coffee spot. Make intentional time each week to reconnect with these anchors. They don't fix the change, but they help you feel safe inside it.

5. Sacred "In-Between" Box

Grab a shoebox or small container. Each week, write down what you're letting go of, and what you're hoping to step into. Fold the papers and place them inside. This becomes your sacred space for transition. A physical act of surrender. A visual reminder that change is a process, and God is in the middle of it.

Change is a disorienting kind of holy. It asks us to step into the unknown. But grace gives us practices to help us feel known, even there.

You don't have to rush. You don't have to be fearless. You just have to be *willing*. One small act of grace at a time.

Reflection Questions

1. **What recent or current life change has stretched you the most?** What emotions, expected or surprising, has it stirred in you?

2. **Where have you felt unprepared or inadequate during this transition?** Can you trace how grace has met you in those vulnerable moments?

3. **What part of your old life or identity are you grieving?** What new part of yourself might be emerging in its place?

4. **Who or what has helped anchor you during change?** How has God used others to remind you that you're not walking alone?

5. **What does it look like to extend grace to yourself in this season?** What can you release today in order to receive peace?

Closing Blessing: Grace for the Transition

May you come to see that change is not a punishment, but a passage.

May you find beauty, even in the unraveling, and courage, even in your trembling steps.

May you stop asking yourself to be perfect and start trusting that showing up, with your open hands and tender heart, is more than enough.

When the road feels unmarked and you feel lost within yourself, may grace rise up to meet you. In the pauses. In the pivots. In the in-between places.

May you remember that you are not behind, not broken, not forgotten. You are in process. You are being made new.

And in this sacred unfolding, God is not watching from a distance. He is walking beside you, holding your hand, whispering, *"I'm making a way in the wilderness. Even now."*

Let that be your peace. Let that be your promise. Let that be your grace.

Amen.

Chapter Nine

♥

"As God's chosen ones, holy and beloved, clothe your-selves with compassion, kindness, humility, meekness, and patience."

Colossians 3:12 (NRSV)

Grace is not just something we receive in our darkest hour; it's the fabric we are meant to wear every day. It's the gentle whisper in the background of chaos, the strength beneath our softness, and the guiding hand that helps us navigate a world that doesn't always reward tenderness. To live a grace-filled life is to live with open hands and an open heart, trusting that we don't have to control everything to be safe, or be perfect to be loved. This chapter invites you into that posture, not just as a moment of reflection, but as a way of life.

Chapter Summary

There's something sacred about a life shaped by grace. It's not flashy. It won't always earn applause or recognition. But it is powerful. A grace-filled life reshapes not only how we move through the world, but how the world experiences us. It touches how we speak to strangers, how we respond when we're wronged, how we hold space for complexity, and how we lean into God when the answers still feel blurry.

This chapter explores what it means to carry grace not just as a reaction to hardship, but as a spiritual practice, a lifestyle, a choice we make every single day. We'll look at the transformation that occurs when grace becomes our lens rather than our last resort. It's about embodying the love of Christ in our tone, our timing, our posture, and our patience.

Living a grace-filled life isn't about smiling through pain or ignoring injustice. It's about choosing presence over performance, people over perfection, and purpose over pride. It's about trusting that we don't need to have all the answers to offer love, and we don't need to be fully healed to help others feel seen. Grace meets us in our becoming, and it walks with us as we become someone who makes space for others to heal too.

Where Grace Met Me: One Messy Tuesday

The moment I realized I was living a grace-filled life didn't come during a church service or some profound mountain-top experience. It came on a Tuesday.

It was one of those days that start with spilled coffee and unravel quietly from there. I had overslept after a night of interrupted sleep. The alarm never went off, or maybe I hit snooze in a fog I couldn't remember. Either way, the day greeted me in full sprint. My son had misplaced one of his shoes, my other son refused to eat the breakfast

I had already made (twice), and my husband and I suffered a massive miscommunication about who was doing morning dropoff.

By 10 a.m., I had already broken down in tears in the hallway, whispering a frustrated prayer: "God, please... just a little peace. Just a little help."

But that wasn't the moment.

The moment came later that afternoon when I opened my laptop to a blinking cursor and a full inbox. I sat frozen for a long time, just staring, no words, no ideas, only the sound of my own breath and the low hum of the washing machine downstairs. I could feel the weight of everything I hadn't done press against me like a judgment. I hadn't followed up on emails. I hadn't prepped dinner. I hadn't made time to call my mother back. And worst of all, I hadn't been "my best self" with my kids or husband that morning.

I could feel the spiral pulling me under.

But then, something shifted. Not because I mustered up some motivational mantra or got a sudden second wind. It was smaller than that. Softer.

I placed my hand on my chest. I closed my eyes. And for the first time that day, I didn't try to fix anything. I didn't try to outpace the failure. I just breathed. I whispered, "This is a grace day."

Not a perfect day. Not even a productive one.

Just a grace day.

A day where the standards I'd set for myself were gently lowered. A day where being present was enough. A day where I could be messy and still loved, overwhelmed and still held, scattered and still sacred.

I stood up, closed the laptop, and sat on the couch with my kids. We watched a cartoon I'd normally groan at. I didn't multitask. I didn't scroll. I just let myself be there.

And when my son leaned his head on my shoulder and said, "Mommy, I like it when you sit still," I felt something holy pass between us.

Grace isn't always grand. Sometimes, it's the decision to be kind to yourself when you feel least deserving. Sometimes it's choosing connection over control. Sometimes, it's turning off the noise and choosing to be human.

I used to think a grace-filled life meant achieving some level of spiritual mastery, being unbothered, endlessly patient, always available. But now I know: a grace-filled life is made in moments like these. Ordinary moments. Messy moments. Moments where we stop striving, and simply choose to rest in the truth that God's love is big enough to meet us exactly where we are.

Not where we wish we were. Not where we think we should be.

But right here, in the living room, in our tired bodies, in our uneven rhythms, on a Tuesday.

Reflection & Spiritual Insight

I used to believe grace was something you chased, something you earned after checking off a long list of spiritual behaviors. I thought living a grace-filled life meant waking up at 5 a.m. to pray, having perfectly filtered words for every tough conversation, keeping my patience intact at all times, and never, *never*, losing my cool. I thought if I could master the right habits, the right posture, the right prayers, then grace would fall upon me like morning dew: refreshing, pure, and earned.

But grace doesn't work like that.

Grace isn't the reward. It's the rhythm.

Living a grace-filled life begins when you stop striving to deserve grace and start receiving it as your baseline. It's not a gold star on a spiritual report card. It's not conditional on your mood, your metrics, or your moral scoreboard. Grace is the breath of God that enters your lungs before you've even spoken His name. It is the reminder that your worth is not defined by your productivity, your emotional regulation, or your ability to "get it all right."

Let that sink in: *you are already living in grace.*

The life of Jesus offers us an invitation, not just to admire His example, but to embody it. And if we really look at how Jesus lived, we'll notice something profound: He moved slowly. He noticed people. He withdrew when He needed to. He was not obsessed with being impressive; He was rooted in being present.

Living a grace-filled life looks less like "doing it all" and more like doing what matters with intention and kindness. It looks like choosing compassion over critique, especially toward yourself. It looks like letting go of your tightly held timeline and trusting God's rhythm. It looks like breathing deeply when your flesh wants to react. It looks like saying "I forgive you" even when the apology never comes. And yes, it looks like laughing with your children when the world outside feels like it's falling apart.

Colossians 3:12 doesn't say, "Clothe yourselves with achievement." It says, "Clothe yourselves with *compassion, kindness, humility, gentleness, and patience.*" These are not passive traits; they're radical postures in a world that worships speed, competition, and perfection. These are spiritual garments that we *choose* to put on, daily.

And here's the truth: there will be days you forget. Days when shame slips on before patience, when irritation beats out compassion, when fear dresses you in pride. That doesn't mean grace is gone. It means grace is needed. And grace, true grace, isn't intimidated by your inconsistency.

God's grace isn't fragile. It's fierce. It holds you when you fumble. It invites you to try again, not because you've failed, but because *He's faithful.*

Living a grace-filled life doesn't mean you never mess up. It means you know where to turn when you do.

It means that when your inner critic shouts "not enough," grace whispers, "I'm still here."

It means when the world says, "Be better," grace says, "Be loved."

It means when you're caught in the chaos, grace anchors you in peace, not because life is tidy, but because God is steady.

Grace transforms everything, not all at once, but little by little, one breath, one choice, one Tuesday at a time.

Related Bible Stories or Characters

One of the clearest biblical examples of what it means to live a grace-filled life is the apostle Paul.

When we think of Paul, we often think of his letters, wise, passionate, bold. We think of the churches he planted, the theology he articulated, the legacy he left. But before he became the messenger of grace, Paul was the very picture of judgment. A man of status, rules, and structure. A persecutor of Christians. Someone who was so confident in his righteousness that he couldn't see how far from grace he actually was.

Until Jesus stopped him. Blinded him. Reached him not through punishment, but through invitation.

In *Acts 9*, we read of Paul's transformation on the road to Damascus, a moment that changed the trajectory of his life. Jesus didn't just correct Paul; He called him. He didn't list all of Paul's wrongdoings;

He simply asked, *"Why are you persecuting me?"* And then, with stunning gentleness, He gave Paul a new assignment.

That is grace.

Not just the kind that forgives, but the kind that restores. The kind that sees beyond who we've been and calls us into who we can become.

From that moment on, Paul didn't just preach about grace; he lived it. He carried it in his body, his letters, his wounds. He described himself as "the worst of sinners" (*1 Timothy 1:15*) and yet also as one "called by the will of God" (*1 Corinthians 1:1*). His life was not perfect or easy, far from it. He faced prison, rejection, hardship, and thorns he begged God to remove. And still, he clung to grace.

In *2 Corinthians 12:9*, Paul shares God's response to his pleading: **"My grace is sufficient for you, for my power is made perfect in weakness."**

Paul's response? *"Therefore I will boast all the more gladly about my weaknesses, so that Christ's power may rest on me."*

That is what a grace-filled life sounds like. Not denial. Not delusion. But the deep knowing that our imperfections do not disqualify us; they make space for God's power to shine.

And Paul didn't just live this way in private. His letters are filled with reminders to the early church about what it means to *walk in grace*:

- To bear with one another in love.

- To speak truth in gentleness.

- To extend forgiveness freely.

- To choose humility over hierarchy.

- To remember that *we have been saved by grace, through faith, not by works, so that no one can boast (Ephesians 2:8–9).*

Paul's story reminds us that a grace-filled life is not a destination we reach; it's a way we move. It's how we respond when we're wronged. How we hold our own past. How we lead, love, and live, even with a limp.

If Paul, once a murderer of Christians, can become the greatest champion of grace, then surely we too can become bearers of that same grace in our homes, in our communities, in our own weary hearts.

Grace doesn't erase our past; it reclaims it.

It turns persecutors into preachers. Failures into vessels. Tired Tuesdays into holy ground.

Gray Space Exploration

It would be much easier if grace came with a checklist.

If there were rules that could guarantee a grace-filled life, many of us would devote ourselves to mastering them. We'd memorize the prayers, perfect the posture, speak the right words, and work endlessly to never disappoint ourselves, or anyone else.

But that's not how grace works. And that's especially not how grace-filled living works.

Living a life steeped in grace doesn't always feel clear-cut. It often takes root in the blurry middle, between the person you used to be and the person you're becoming. Between the life you dreamed of and the one you're navigating now. Between what your faith tells you is true and what your emotions are screaming in the moment.

The gray space is where grace gets real.

Because here's the honest truth: sometimes grace doesn't look like strength. Sometimes it looks like boundaries that make you feel guilty.

Sometimes it looks like saying "no" even when everything in you wants to people-please. Sometimes it means holding space for your own mess without needing to rush into a fix.

Sometimes, the most grace-filled choice is not the prettiest one.

Like when you choose not to return a phone call right away, not because you don't care, but because you know you're not in a place to offer love instead of resentment.

Or when you give yourself permission to rest instead of forcing productivity, knowing full well the world will label that as lazy.

Or when you forgive someone who never apologized, not because what they did was okay, but because you're tired of carrying bitterness like a second skin.

Grace doesn't always make sense on paper.

That's why it lives in the gray.

The truth is, we are constantly navigating tension: being faithful and being frustrated, being hopeful and being honest about our doubts. We're not static beings; we're in process. And grace doesn't skip over that process; it enters it.

Living a grace-filled life in the gray means learning to ask better questions: "Where is love guiding me?" instead of "What will make me look holy?" "What does my soul need today?" instead of "How do I stay ahead?" "How can I show up fully?" instead of "How can I prove I'm enough?"

In this space, grace teaches us to be okay with not having a clear answer. It teaches us to rest in God's presence, even when we're unsure of our own. It teaches us that tension isn't failure; it's formation.

And perhaps the greatest act of grace is learning to trust that God still calls us worthy, even while we're in the gray.

Connection to Reader's Life

Maybe you're here because you're tired.

Tired of trying to be the strong one. Tired of always knowing the right answer. Tired of carrying the emotional weight for everyone else. Tired of holding it together when what you really want is to fall apart, just for a moment, just to see if the world would still keep spinning.

Maybe you've spent your whole life striving. Maybe "grace" is a word you've heard in sermons and songs, but not one you've ever really believed could belong to *you*. Maybe you've been waiting to feel spiritual enough, calm enough, *good* enough to claim a life steeped in it.

But friend, grace is not for the polished. It's for the in-progress.

You don't need a five-year plan to live a grace-filled life. You don't need to master spiritual disciplines or live in a monastery. You don't have to be the most patient mom, the most forgiving daughter, the most understanding spouse, the most gracious coworker. You just need to begin, right here, right now, by saying, "Even in this, I am still loved."

A grace-filled life isn't something you wake up and find one morning like a prize waiting on your doorstep. It's something you *build*, moment by moment. It's in the quiet decision to take a breath instead of snapping back. It's in the choice to offer your reflection a soft smile instead of a sigh of disappointment. It's in the radical act of saying "I forgive you" when bitterness would feel easier.

Grace doesn't ask you to erase your edges. It asks you to bring them to God.

Living this way doesn't mean life gets easier; it just means your soul breathes deeper. It means you begin to treat yourself the way God has always treated you: with kindness, compassion, and the deep belief that you are not too far gone. You are not behind. You are not broken beyond repair.

You are becoming.

So if you're the one who wakes up some mornings already feeling behind... If you're the one who feels like you're failing at "balance"... If you're the one who gives everyone else grace but doesn't know how to offer it inward...

You are not disqualified.

You are exactly where grace can meet you.

And just like you don't have to understand how the sun rises to trust that it will, you don't have to know all the steps to begin living this way. Start small. Start soft. Start today.

Because the world needs more grace-filled people. Not perfect people. Not polished people.

Just people who are willing to choose love over performance, again and again.

Practical Application / Tools for Grace

Living a grace-filled life is less about getting it right and more about getting real. It's the slow, sacred work of choosing compassion when frustration knocks. It's learning to lean into love when shame tries to take the mic. Below are a few gentle, grounding tools to help you embody grace, not just in theory, but in practice.

1. The Morning Mirror Ritual

Each morning, look yourself in the mirror, not with critique, but with curiosity. Whisper aloud:

"I am worthy of grace today. Not because of what I do, but because of who I am in God."

This isn't about vanity. It's about *visibility*. Seeing yourself as God sees you. Let this be your daily armor: not performance, but presence.

2. The "Pause and Breathe" Practice

When you're on the verge of spiraling, whether from overwhelm, frustration, or self-criticism, pause and place a hand over your heart. Close your eyes. Breathe in slowly for 4 counts, hold for 4, exhale for 6.

Whisper this breath prayer:

Inhale: *"Your grace is enough..."* Exhale: *"...even now."*

Let this breath become your reset button, an invitation back to God's peace.

3. The Grace Inventory (Weekly Practice)

Once a week, sit down with a journal or a voice memo app and reflect:

- Where did I extend grace to others this week?

- Where did I withhold it, from myself or someone else?

- What moment reminded me that I'm still learning, and that's okay?

This is not an evaluation. It's an embrace.

4. A Grace-Filled Phone Note

Create a running note on your phone titled *"Proof of Grace."* Throughout the week, jot down anything that feels like grace:

- A kind text you didn't expect.

- The courage to say no.

- A moment where you breathed before reacting.

- A burst of laughter in the middle of a hard day.

Watch the list grow. You'll start to notice: grace was everywhere.

5. The "Bare Minimum" Day

When you're exhausted, overwhelmed, or deep in self-doubt, declare a "bare minimum day." Not out of laziness, but out of love. This is your permission slip to *release the pressure* and just do what's necessary:

- Eat something nourishing.

- Send one important email.

- Take a shower or sit in the sun.

- Say, "That's enough for today."

Grace means your worth isn't measured by your output.

6. Extend Grace Out Loud

Pick one person each week to intentionally extend grace toward. A friend who's been distant. A partner who's had a rough week. A child who is learning. Yourself.

Say it. Text it. Show it.

"I see you trying. That's enough." "You don't have to be perfect to be loved." "I forgive you. We're still good."

The more you practice saying these things to others, the easier it becomes to believe them for yourself.

Grace doesn't have to be loud. It doesn't have to be poetic. It just has to be *present*.

And if you keep showing up, messy, tired, healing, trying, grace will meet you there. Every single time.

Reflection Questions

Take a quiet moment, whether it's curled up on the couch, sitting under a blanket of stars, or tucked away in a corner with your journal, and let these questions lead you into stillness, honesty, and sacred self-awareness. These aren't tests. They're doorways.

1. What does a grace-filled life look like *for you*, not just in theory, but in your real, everyday rhythms?

How would your mornings feel? How would you speak to yourself in the mirror? What would shift in the way you show up for others?

2. Where in your life do you feel most tempted to perform, prove, or perfect?

What would it feel like to lay that burden down and trust that *you are enough, even here*?

3. When was the last time you extended grace to someone else? How did it feel?

Now flip it: when was the last time you extended that same level of grace to *yourself*?

4. What inner script or belief is making it hard for you to live a grace-filled life right now?

Is there a voice inside you that says, "You should be further along"? What would it sound like to let God's voice be louder than that?

5. Who models a grace-filled life to you?

Think of someone in your life (or a public figure or even a character in Scripture) who lives with softness, strength, and deep compassion. What do they *do* differently? What *mindset* might they have that you can begin to adopt?

Optional Journal Prompt: "If I gave myself the same grace I give to the people I love most, my life would begin to feel like..."

Closing Blessing

May your life become a sanctuary of grace.

Not because everything is tidy or calm, but because you have learned how to live gently, with yourself and with others. May your days be wrapped in compassion, your words clothed in kindness, your failures met with forgiveness, and your joys deepened by gratitude.

May you wake up and remember that grace is not something you earn; it's something you already carry. May it flow from you not through effort, but through overflow.

When you feel hurried, may grace slow your pace.

When you feel unworthy, may grace whisper, "You are still mine."

When the world demands performance, may you choose presence.

And on the days you forget, on the days when you snap, spiral, sink, or stray, may grace find you again. Because it always does.

You don't have to be perfect to live a grace-filled life. You just have to keep choosing love, one small moment at a time.

Amen.

Chapter Ten

♥

"And God is able to provide you with every blessing in abundance, so that by always having enough of everything, you may share abundantly in every good work."

2 Corinthians 9:8 (NRSV)

Before the Waves Reach the Shore...

Pause with me for a moment.

Close your eyes, if you can, and picture a still pond. The surface is calm, quiet, undisturbed. Then, imagine tossing in the smallest of pebbles. Watch as the ripples spread, widening slowly but steadily, touching everything in their path. That's what grace does. It starts in a single moment, a kind word, a second chance, an unexpected act of kindness, and expands outward, reaching places and people we may never see.

Grace doesn't just stop with us. It flows through us.

It's not confined to a private moment or a quiet prayer. It shows up in classrooms and kitchens, across dinner tables and text messages, in the way we respond to rudeness or forgive an old wound. Grace creates motion, holy, healing motion, that changes not just us, but everyone we come into contact with.

And sometimes, the smallest ripple creates the most beautiful shift.

Chapter Summary

This chapter is about how grace doesn't stay still; it moves, multiplies, and makes waves. When we choose to extend grace, even in the tiniest ways, we unknowingly initiate a domino effect of healing and connection. The spiritual tension here is the question we often ask ourselves: *"What difference can I really make?"* In a world brimming with chaos and conflict, our individual acts of grace can feel small, even insignificant.

But God's economy works differently. He multiplies the seed.

This chapter explores the quiet power of grace in motion. We'll dive into stories where kindness echoed further than expected, examine how forgiveness shifts atmospheres, and reflect on the spiritual principle that when we act in grace, we're participating in a divine cycle far bigger than ourselves.

You'll see how one moment of grace can soften a hardened heart, mend a fractured relationship, or even inspire a stranger to pass on the same kindness. Grace, when released, is contagious. It spreads. And it always comes back full circle.

Where Grace Met Me: A Muffin, A Mess, and a Miracle

It all started with a blueberry muffin.

Not a homemade, Pinterest-worthy muffin. I'm talking about a slightly stale, gas-station kind of muffin, the kind sealed in plastic wrap and stuffed into a convenience store display next to the beef jerky and half-forgotten lottery tickets.

I was running late that morning, late for a meeting, late for life, really. You know those mornings where everything is off? The kind where your coffee spills down the front of your shirt *right* as you reach for your keys, only to realize they're not in your purse, but somehow inside the refrigerator? That was my morning.

I had managed to scrape myself together just enough to throw on a blazer, touch up the coffee stain with a baby wipe, and grab the cheapest muffin I could find on my way to the office. I felt frazzled, defeated, and honestly, like a hot mess. As I pulled into the office parking lot, I took a deep breath and said one of those "Jesus, take the wheel" prayers. And with that, I slipped on my heels, grabbed my purse, and opened the door.

Only, the muffin had other plans.

Somehow, in the rush, I had balanced the muffin on top of my folder, which immediately slid off and fell, splat, right into the parking lot puddle. Now, there's no delicate way to say this: I cried over that muffin. Right there in the parking lot. Standing in heels, hair frizzing in the humidity, watching my sad breakfast float away like a soggy boat of defeat.

That's when it happened.

Out of nowhere, a woman I had never seen before walked over, holding a white paper bag and a coffee tray.

"You okay?" she asked gently, as if I were a wounded bird and not a grown woman mourning baked goods.

"I'm fine," I lied through a sniffle. "Just... muffin problems."

She smiled, one of those real, crinkly-eyed smiles that don't pity you, but somehow see you. "Well, I got an extra this morning," she said, reaching into the bag. "Blueberry. You want it?"

I stared at her like she was an angel in yoga pants and sneakers.

She handed it to me, still warm from the bakery down the street. I tried to protest, to explain that I couldn't take her breakfast, but she just shrugged. "Someone did this for me last week. I'm just paying it forward."

And with that, she walked away.

The muffin tasted like heaven. But what stuck with me more was the grace in that moment. That stranger didn't know what kind of morning I was having. She didn't know how deeply overwhelmed I'd felt lately, how I was questioning my purpose, feeling like I was failing at all the important things. She didn't know that I had barely made it through the week without crumbling. But she saw me in that silly, soggy moment and extended grace.

That one gesture shifted something in me.

Later that afternoon, I bought lunch for a colleague who had forgotten hers. That evening, I sent a "just because" text to a friend I hadn't spoken to in months. And the next day, I brought an extra muffin to the office, just in case someone else needed one.

Here's the thing: grace ripples.

It starts in the smallest acts, the unnoticed, uncelebrated, seemingly random ones, and it multiplies. It flows from one heart to the next, transforming ordinary days into sacred spaces.

All because someone shared a muffin and a moment of kindness in a parking lot.

Reflection & Spiritual Insight: The Grace We Pass Along

I used to think grace had to be grand.

You know, the kind of grace that shows up in sweeping gestures. A tearful reconciliation at the altar. A life-altering miracle. A dramatic, goosebump-worthy moment that people write worship songs about. But the more life I live, the more I realize that grace is often *quiet*. It's in the margin. In the seemingly insignificant. In the $3 muffin and the stranger who stopped to see me, not as a burden or an inconvenience, but as a human being worthy of care.

That moment taught me something profound: **grace doesn't always look like rescue—it often looks like recognition**.

In 2 Corinthians 9:8, Paul reminds us, *"And God is able to bless you abundantly, so that in all things at all times, having all that you need, you will abound in every good work."* God equips us with grace not just to survive, but to *give*. Not just to receive comfort, but to be a source of it for someone else.

I didn't know it at the time, but I was on the receiving end of what I now call a "grace ripple." Someone else had poured kindness into this stranger's life. She caught that wave and passed it to me. I felt seen in my mess, and from that small spark of compassion, I began to see others differently too. I carried the warmth of that moment into every interaction that followed. My heart was softer. My words were gentler. My patience deepened.

It's easy to underestimate those little things. A smile in a hallway. A call to check on someone. Covering the cost of a coffee. They may seem insignificant, but they carry **weight**. They can *rewire* someone's day, *rebuild* their sense of worth, and *remind* them that they are not alone.

Sometimes, we wait to offer grace until we feel "qualified." Until we've got our own life together. Until we're stronger, wiser, more spiritual. But what if grace flows best when we stop trying to qualify ourselves and just *show up*? That woman didn't know my name, my story, or what I needed spiritually. But she had *extra*. And she offered it.

That's what grace is. The *overflow*.

It's not a reservoir; it's a current. It doesn't stop with us. It moves through us. And when we allow ourselves to be vessels of grace, however messy or imperfect we may feel, we become part of a divine chain reaction.

And isn't that just like God?

He doesn't wait until we have it all figured out. He meets us in parking lots. In soggy muffin moments. In random kindnesses and gentle nudges. He uses the ordinary to do something extraordinary. And He invites us to do the same.

You don't need a platform to make an impact. You just need a heart willing to say, "Here's what I have. Take it. I've got a little extra today."

Related Bible Story: The Grace of the Good Samaritan

One of the most well-known parables Jesus ever told was in response to a simple but profound question: *"And who is my neighbor?"* (Luke 10:29). His answer wasn't a theological treatise or a philosophical explanation; it was a story. A story about **a ripple of grace**.

A man is attacked on the road from Jerusalem to Jericho, robbed, stripped, and left for dead. Two religious leaders, a priest and a Levite, pass by without helping. They had their reasons, we're sure. They may have been late for temple duties. They may have feared for their safety. But whatever the reason, they passed by a hurting man without stopping.

Then came the Samaritan.

Someone from a group historically at odds with Jews. Someone with *every reason* to keep walking. But instead, he stopped. He bound the man's wounds. He placed him on his own donkey. He brought him to an inn, paid for his stay, and even left instructions for future care.

Here's what makes that moment a ripple: **the Samaritan's grace didn't stop at the roadside. It carried forward.** It influenced the innkeeper. It challenged the assumptions of everyone listening to Jesus. And now, thousands of years later, it challenges *us*. That one man's act of grace has rippled across centuries.

He didn't help because he had to. He helped because he saw someone in need, and he allowed himself to be moved.

Isn't that the heart of grace?

It's not limited by our labels or our categories. It sees the humanity in others and acts out of compassion. It disrupts the flow of judgment and replaces it with healing. And just like that Samaritan, we don't need status or spiritual credentials to change someone's life. We just need a willingness to stop.

To offer what we have.

To notice the hurting.

To start a ripple.

That's the grace Jesus modeled, and that's the grace He calls us to extend.

Gray Space Exploration: When Grace Isn't Convenient

Here's the thing about grace; it rarely shows up when it's convenient.

We like to imagine ourselves as people who would stop on the side of the road, who would offer the extra muffin, who would forgive easily. But real life is more complicated than that.

Sometimes the person in need of our grace is the coworker who keeps missing deadlines and making *us* look bad. Sometimes it's the family member who *never apologizes,* or the friend who disappeared when we needed them most. Sometimes the person needing grace is *us*, when we've messed up, lashed out, let someone down, or simply run out of emotional energy.

Grace lives in the tension.

It lives in the moment you want to say, "They don't deserve this," and the quiet whisper of God says, "Neither did you, but I gave it anyway."

It's that uncomfortable, fuzzy space between your justified frustration and your higher calling. It's not black-and-white. Grace doesn't always mean letting someone off the hook or denying your own boundaries. But it *does* mean looking at people through a lens of compassion, even when your ego or your pain is screaming for revenge.

And sometimes, let's be honest, grace feels unfair.

It feels like letting someone "get away with it." It feels like choosing vulnerability in a world that rewards defense. It feels like trusting God with the outcome, even when you don't get to see how the story ends.

That's the gray.

Grace asks us to step into that foggy middle ground, where the lines between right and wrong aren't so clear, where the emotions are messy, and where we can't always predict what the "ripple" will be.

But that's also where God does His best work.

In the parking lot moments.

In the late-night phone calls.

In the act of forgiveness that no one applauds.

In the anonymous gift.

In the unseen kindness.

The ripple effect of grace doesn't need a stage. It just needs your *yes*. Even when it's blurry. Even when it's hard. Even when it's gray.

Connection to Reader's Life: You Are Someone's Ripple

Let's be honest, most of us don't feel like we're doing something world-changing on a Tuesday morning. We're just trying to get the kids out the door without anyone crying (including us), answer emails without losing our minds, and maybe, *maybe*, remember to drink water. Life can feel like one long to-do list. Who has time to think about grace?

But that's the beauty of it.

Grace doesn't require you to rearrange your life. It asks you to *notice* it inside your life.

That smile you offered the grocery clerk who looked like she was barely holding it together? That mattered. The time you forgave your partner even though they didn't say the perfect words? That mattered. The moment you didn't snap back when you *really* wanted to? That mattered.

These are the tiny, sacred decisions that change people.

You may never know how your kindness redirected someone's entire day, or their life. But grace never goes to waste. Even when it feels invisible. Even when it feels small.

And sometimes, the one who needs your grace most... is *you*.

Maybe you're the one feeling behind. Maybe you've been holding on to shame, to guilt, to the memory of something you wish you had handled better. Maybe you're still waiting for someone to extend grace to *you*, and that absence has left a tender bruise.

Please hear this: **you are not disqualified**.

God's grace reaches you, even here.

And in the same way that woman's muffin made me feel human again, your softness with yourself may be the beginning of your own ripple. When we allow ourselves to be loved, held, forgiven, we're more likely to do the same for others.

That's the invitation: to be a *carrier* of grace.

Not because you have it all together. But because you *know* what it's like to fall apart, and be loved anyway.

So, today, ask yourself:

Who needs your grace? Where can you sow a seed of kindness, even if you don't see the harvest? How might your ordinary life become someone else's answered prayer?

You are already creating ripples, more than you know.

Practical Application / Tools for Grace

Creating Ripples on Purpose

Grace doesn't always need to be spontaneous. Sometimes, it's something we *choose*, with forethought, intention, and holy creativity. Here are some practical ways to extend grace and multiply its impact, creating ripples that go farther than you could ever imagine:

1. Start a "Grace List"

Each week, write down three ways someone showed you grace, no matter how small. Then write down three ways you could pay that grace forward. This small ritual builds awareness and intention. Keep the list somewhere you'll see it, on the fridge, your bathroom mirror, or in your journal.

2. Grace in a Mug

The next time you grab coffee, pay for the person behind you. Simple? Yes. But surprisingly powerful. That $4 act of kindness might hit someone on their lowest day. Bonus ripple: Leave a little note for the barista with words like "You matter" or "You're doing amazing." They'll feel it too.

3. Use Your Words as Water

Speak life into someone who's been shrinking lately. Text that friend you haven't heard from. Compliment your coworker not for their output, but for their presence. Tell your kid, "I love who you are," not just "I'm proud of what you did." Let your words be a balm; they might be the only kind ones that person hears today.

4. Silent Grace

Sometimes grace looks like saying *nothing* at all, choosing not to correct someone, not pointing out the mistake, not demanding the apology. Silent grace is a powerful ripple. It honors the space someone needs to grow without shame.

5. The Grace Basket

Create a small basket in your home or workplace with comforting items, snacks, tissues, notes of encouragement, lotion, tea bags. Invite others to take what they need or leave something behind. This tangible grace becomes a collective ripple that lives on and on.

6. Mirror Check

Every time you look in the mirror, instead of criticizing yourself, speak this aloud:

"I am worthy of grace. I carry it. I give it. I live in it."

It's hard to create ripples outward when we don't honor grace inward. Let your self-talk reflect the truth of God's love for you.

7. Grace Challenge of the Week

Choose one person who irritates you, or who you've been quietly avoiding, and do one kind thing for them this week. It could be a compliment, a thoughtful gesture, or just a soft word when you'd normally withdraw. It's not about faking it. It's about choosing to live *beyond the offense*. Grace stretches us, and that's how we grow.

These tools aren't about performance. They're about presence.

Grace doesn't demand perfection; it asks for availability. And when we show up with even the smallest offering, God turns it into more than we could ever imagine.

Reflection Questions: Stirring the Waters of Grace

1. **When was the last time someone showed you grace in a way that surprised you?** What did it teach you about the power of small acts?

2. **Can you remember a time when *you* extended grace, and it shifted the atmosphere or a relationship?** How did that moment ripple outward, whether or not you saw the result?

3. **Where in your life right now do you feel called to create a ripple of grace?** Is there a relationship, space, or situation that could benefit from your compassion?

4. **What's one way you can become more aware of grace in the "small things"?** How might this awareness shape your mindset and daily choices?

5. **Have you been resisting grace for yourself or others?** What would it look like to lay that resistance down, and to let grace move freely through you?

Closing Blessing: May Your Grace Ripple Wide

May you never underestimate the quiet power of your presence. May you know that even the smallest act of kindness can echo through eternity. May you recognize that grace is not a performance, but a posture, a willingness to see others, and yourself, through the eyes of love.

When your day feels ordinary, may you remember: that's often where God does His most extraordinary work. When you feel unseen, may someone's ripple reach you. And when you are overflowing, may you become someone's miracle.

Let your life be a gentle current of compassion, a wave of grace that starts in your heart and flows outward, touching one life, then another, then another still.

You are already part of the ripple. Now, go make waves.

Amen.

Final Reflections

♥

"Let us therefore approach the throne of grace with boldness, so that we may receive mercy and find grace to help in time of need."

Hebrews 4:16 (NRSV)

Themed Meditation

There's something deeply sacred about looking back, not with shame or regret, but with reverence. As if each scar, each unanswered prayer, and each unexpected blessing formed a mosaic too intricate to understand in the moment. And yet, somehow, grace was always there. It whispered through the losses, lingered in the laughter, and anchored us when nothing else could. As we reach the end of this journey through the blurry, the gray, and the broken, this moment asks something different of us, not action, not understanding, but reflection. To pause. To breathe. To let the fullness of grace settle into the marrow of our bones. To believe, with quiet confidence, that the same grace that carried us this far will continue to carry us home.

Chapter Summary

This final chapter is an invitation. Not into something new, but into something deeper, a recognition that grace has been the undercurrent of every chapter of our lives, even when we didn't know how to name it. We've traced its presence through suffering, transformation, uncertainty, relationships, and healing. We've witnessed how grace moves, slow and subtle at times, fierce and freeing at others.

But grace doesn't retire when the story ends. It continues. It evolves. It becomes a way of life.

This chapter offers space to look at our entire journey, not just the pages of this book, but the unwritten stories of our own lives, and ask: How has grace transformed me? Where do I still need it? And how can I live in a way that reflects its constant invitation?

We are not the same as when we began. We are softer, perhaps. Wiser. Maybe a little more tender with our own hearts and the hearts of others. That is grace at work. Not fixing us. But shaping us. Holding us. Reminding us that our humanity was never the problem; it was always part of the plan.

Where Grace Met Me: Grace in the Full Picture

There's a certain stillness that comes at the end of a long, hard journey. Not the kind of stillness that screams "rest" from the rooftops, but the

kind that whispers, *"You made it through."* And for me, that whisper
came on a seemingly ordinary Tuesday morning.

The sun had barely climbed above the horizon, casting its sleepy
orange glow across my kitchen floor. The house was quiet, the kind of
quiet that feels sacred, like a hush before something holy. My son was
still tucked into the folds of his favorite nook, my daughter curled up
with her head nestled in her favorite pillow, snoring softly.. And me? I
was standing at the sink, gripping my coffee mug with both hands, as
if holding on to that warm ceramic vessel could keep the weight of the
world from spilling over.

It had been a week. One of those weeks. The kind where parenting
felt like walking barefoot on gravel, and marriage felt like trying to tune
into a radio station that kept fading in and out. My body was tired.
My spirit was even more so. But there, in the quiet glow of morning,
something inside me softened.

I glanced up at the refrigerator, cluttered with drawings, family
pictures, appointment reminders, and old baby pictures, and I saw it:
the wrinkled ultrasound photo from my first pregnancy. The one we
lost.

It had been months since I'd given it more than a passing glance, but
this morning, it called to me. Not in grief, not in pain, but in gratitude.

Tears welled up before I even realized what was happening. And not
the kind of tears that burn your throat with anger or sorrow. These
were warm, gentle tears. The kind that only come when your heart is
full to the brim with something too holy for words.

Because standing in that kitchen, surrounded by a life I once
thought I'd never have, I felt the full weight of grace.

I remembered the teenage version of myself, lying on a sterile exam
table, blinking back tears as a doctor explained the complex condition
of my uterus, then handed me paperwork for a hysterectomy before I

could legally drink. I remembered the heartbreak of dating men who would never see me as worthy of motherhood, and the ache of loving children who would never call me "Mom."

I remembered the crushing silence after my first miscarriage, the way I'd curled up on the bathroom floor, cradling a pain too big for words. I remembered shouting at God in the dark, accusing Him of betrayal, of cruelty, of dangling hope like a carrot on a string. And I remembered the second pink line on the pregnancy test that followed months later, the one I didn't even trust at first, afraid it would vanish like a cruel joke.

But now, looking around my home, I saw it all so differently.

The clutter. The chaos. The stickiness of peanut butter smudged across the counter. The faint smell of lavender baby shampoo clinging to the air. The 3 week-old dried up roses brought by my husband just because he loves me. These weren't messes. These were miracles.

I smiled through my tears and whispered to no one in particular, "It was all grace. Every bit of it."

Not just the blessings. Not just the victories or the answered prayers. But the long nights of waiting. The therapy appointments. The hard conversations. The quiet moments of despair. The stretch marks, on my body and on my soul. All of it. Grace in disguise.

I think we often look for grace in the polished moments. The triumphs. The testimonies that wrap up nicely with a bow. But that morning, I knew: grace had been with me in the blurry middle, in the fumbling prayers, and in the long, uncertain seasons when nothing made sense.

It was there when I felt unworthy and unloved. It was there when I pushed people away and when I clung too tightly. It was there in the friends who didn't know what to say but showed up anyway, and in the family who kept loving me through every low and every loud silence.

And most of all, grace was there in *me*, as I kept getting up, kept trying again, kept choosing love even when I didn't feel whole enough to give it.

That's the thing no one tells you. Grace isn't just something that finds you; it's something you learn to recognize. To receive. To rest in. And once you do, it rewrites how you see your past and how you move through your future.

Because grace doesn't always look like a breakthrough or a miracle on paper. Sometimes, it looks like a tired woman in an old bathrobe, sipping coffee in a quiet kitchen, looking at her cluttered refrigerator and realizing that her life, messy, imperfect, and profoundly sacred, is the very proof that grace was always enough.

Reflection & Spiritual Insight: Grace is the Thread That Holds It All

There's a moment in every journey when you look back, not just to see how far you've come, but to truly *see* what carried you. What allowed you to keep walking when the road felt like it would swallow you whole. And for me, that moment of quiet revelation in my kitchen was more than a personal victory. It was a spiritual awakening.

I saw how grace didn't just appear at the end of the story like a ribbon wrapped around a hard season. It was the thread that had been pulling me forward all along. It wasn't just in the final blessing; it was in the battle, in the breakdown, in the breathless moments when I wasn't sure I could continue.

Grace had always been there. And now I could finally see it.

Isn't that just like God?

He doesn't always shout His presence. Sometimes, He whispers it. Through a quiet sunrise. A crinkled ultrasound photo. A child's laugh echoing down the hallway. A scripture you've read a thousand times, but suddenly feels like it was written just for you today.

Grace is not something we earn. It's not a reward for our strength or our obedience. It's the evidence of God's heart toward us, unwavering, unrelenting, and wildly compassionate. And it shows up most clearly not when we are polished and put together, but when we're unraveling. When we're not sure we deserve anything but silence, and instead, He gives us mercy.

I think of 2 Corinthians 12:9 again and again:

"My grace is sufficient for you, for my power is made perfect in weakness."

Not in control. Not in our wisdom. Not in our five-year plans.

In weakness.

That verse is a paradox and a promise. It tells us that our most fragile moments are often the most powerful. Because it's in those places, those raw, exposed, trembling places, that God can finally get close. That we let Him in, not as a cosmic fixer, but as a tender Father who sits with us in the middle of the mess.

I used to think that a grace-filled life meant always being kind, always having answers, always moving forward with purpose. But now I know better. A grace-filled life is one that makes room, for tears and laughter, for doubt and faith, for sorrow and joy.

It's one that doesn't force healing to look like perfection. It allows healing to look like presence.

God's grace didn't eliminate my pain, but it redefined it. It turned wounds into wisdom. It softened my heart toward others. It gave me the courage to love myself, even when I didn't feel lovable. It helped me forgive, not just others, but the version of me that didn't know any better yet. The one who tried, failed, broke down, got back up, and tried again.

That, dear reader, is grace in motion.

If you're standing in a moment right now that feels too complicated, too heavy, or too far gone to be touched by grace, I want you to pause and hear this:

God is not waiting for you to be perfect. He's not waiting for you to "get it together." He's already there. In the in-between. In the blurry. In the breath you just took. And His grace? It is sufficient. For *this* moment. And the next one. And the one after that.

So if nothing else today, let your soul exhale. You are not alone. You are not disqualified. You are being held. And you are being remade, moment by moment, by a grace that never gives up on you.

Related Bible Stories or Characters: Peter – From Denial to Devotion

If there's one figure in Scripture who embodies the long arc of transformation through grace, it's Peter.

Peter, the bold. Peter, the impulsive. Peter, the one who swore he'd never abandon Jesus... only to do exactly that, not once, but three times in the very hour Jesus needed him most.

Let that sink in. This wasn't a stranger. This wasn't a lukewarm follower. This was one of Jesus' closest friends, one of the first disciples called, the one who walked on water and witnessed miracles up close. And yet, in a moment of fear, Peter denied even knowing Him.

Three denials. Three betrayals. And still, Jesus came back for him.

After the resurrection, Jesus didn't return to Peter with a lecture. He didn't list his failures or demand an apology. Instead, He cooked him breakfast on the shore. A quiet fire. Some fish. A meal shared not in punishment, but in love.

And then, Jesus asked him three simple questions: "Peter, do you love me?" Not once. Not twice. But three times, one for every denial.

This wasn't shame. This was redemption in slow motion. This was grace, personalized. Jesus wasn't just forgiving Peter; He was re-commissioning him. Restoring him. Giving him back his purpose.

"Feed my sheep," He said. In other words: *You're still mine. I still trust you. You still belong.*

What strikes me most about Peter's story is not his failure, but what came after. Peter didn't let his shame silence him. Grace allowed him to rise. To become the rock upon which the church was built. To preach boldly. To lead. To love.

Peter's journey reminds us that grace doesn't cancel our calling. It revives it.

So many of us walk through seasons where we feel we've messed up too badly, wandered too far, doubted too deeply. But Peter's story tells us: **even our worst moments can become the soil for our greatest growth**.

Like Peter, I've denied the truth of who I am in moments of fear. I've questioned God's goodness. I've run from what I knew was right because it felt safer than risking disappointment again.

But also like Peter, I've been met with grace on the shorelines of my shame.

I've felt Jesus sit beside me, not with condemnation, but with breakfast. With presence. With a quiet voice asking, *Do you still love Me?*

And the truth is: I do.

So I keep showing up. With my flaws. With my failures. With my heart cracked wide open for grace to do what only grace can do, make beauty out of the brokenness.

And just like Peter, I've learned: God's grace isn't just about second chances. It's about never running out of them.

Gray Space Exploration: The In-Between is Holy, Too

We like our stories neat. We crave resolution, closure, clean lines between good and bad, right and wrong. But life rarely unfolds in a straight line. Most of it happens in the in-between.

There were so many seasons in my life that didn't tie up with a ribbon. Chapters that closed with a question mark instead of a period.

Moments when the apology never came. Relationships that didn't heal the way I prayed they would. Doors that stayed shut, without explanation. Joys that were tinged with sorrow. Victories that came too late to celebrate the way I once imagined.

There were times I showed grace and it wasn't returned. Times I received grace and didn't feel I deserved it. Times I thought I was healed only to find another layer of hurt still waiting quietly underneath.

That's the gray space.

It's the place where your faith is strong, but your knees are still shaking. Where you love people who don't change. Where you forgive, not because it makes everything better, but because it makes *you* better. Where you hold grief and gratitude in the same breath. Where you don't know what comes next, but you show up anyway.

The truth is, grace thrives in that gray.

Because grace doesn't need things to make sense in order to be real. It doesn't require an ending to start working. It just needs your "yes" in the middle of the mess.

We don't often talk about the spiritual richness of unresolved stories. But maybe we should.

Because it's in those stories where we learn to see people as people, not as villains or heroes. It's where we learn to hold tension without needing to fix it. It's where we find the divine not in certainty, but in surrender.

For me, grace didn't wait for me to become whole. It met me while I was unraveling. It whispered truth when all I could see was contradiction. It reminded me that healing doesn't mean forgetting; it means learning to carry your story with softness.

And I wonder if maybe that's the whole point.

Not to wrap life up in a pretty bow. Not to solve every mystery. But to keep walking through the gray with courage, compassion, and the quiet confidence that grace is not just at the end of the road; it's in every step along the way.

So if your life doesn't look like a highlight reel... If your faith feels complicated... If your healing is unfinished... You're not doing it wrong. You're just living in the gray.

And that, dear reader, is sacred ground.

Connection to Reader's Life: Your Life Is Worthy of Grace, Too

Take a deep breath, friend.

Really, breathe in. Let it fill your lungs slowly. And now exhale. Let your shoulders fall. Let your heart settle. Because this part? This is for you.

I wonder what grace has looked like in your story.

Maybe you've read these pages nodding along with tears in your eyes, thinking, *Yes... that sounds like me.* Or maybe you've flipped through this book feeling a quiet ache, a longing for something you're not sure you've ever experienced.

Either way, I want you to know this: **you are not behind. You are not forgotten. And you are not too messy for grace.**

Maybe you've survived a season that no one else knows about. Maybe you've smiled through silent grief or poured yourself into everyone else while secretly wondering if anyone sees *you*. Maybe you've carried shame like a secret language, one you speak fluently in your own mind but hide from the world.

Or maybe... you've just grown weary.

Of pretending. Of pushing. Of wondering when it's your turn to feel whole again.

Here's what I want you to consider: **grace has already been showing up for you.**

Maybe it was in the friend who texted you "just thinking of you" on a day you needed it most. Maybe it was the moment you finally said "no" without apologizing. Maybe it was in the song that came on the radio at just the right time, or the breath you took after a long cry when you finally realized, *I'm still here.*

Sometimes grace isn't loud or dramatic. Sometimes it looks like survival. Like softness where you used to be sharp. Like boundaries that protect your heart. Like allowing yourself to be loved in the middle of your healing.

And if you're not there yet, if you still feel tangled up in regret, doubt, or disappointment, I want to lovingly remind you: **this isn't the end of your story.**

You don't have to clean up before grace comes. You don't have to explain your way into worthiness. You don't have to figure it all out before you let yourself rest in love.

God's grace is not limited to mountaintop moments. It's in the hallway where you're waiting for the next door to open. It's in the car ride home after the hard conversation. It's in the quiet resolve to try again. To stay. To hope. To breathe.

So ask yourself, softly:

- Where has grace shown up in my life when I didn't realize it?

- What parts of my story still feel too heavy to hold?

- Can I let go of the need to make it all make sense, and just let grace meet me here?

You don't have to be perfect. You just have to be present.

And maybe that's the most radical act of grace: **choosing to stay in your story, exactly as you are.** Not because it's easy. But because you're worthy of the love that's waiting for you.

Right here. Right now. In the gray.

Practical Application / Tools for Grace: Living It Forward

By now, you've probably realized that grace isn't just an idea; it's a *practice.* It's a lens. A lifestyle. A quiet revolution in how we live, love, and lead ourselves through the uncertain.

Here are a few sacred, soul-soothing ways to continue your grace journey beyond these pages:

1. Create a "Grace Timeline"

Take a moment to reflect on the seasons of your life, especially the blurry, the hard, the unfinished. Draw a simple timeline, and mark the major moments: heartbreaks, breakthroughs, transitions, losses, wins. Then next to each, ask:

- *How did grace show up here, even if subtly?*

- *Who or what carried me through?*

- *What did I learn about myself and God in this chapter?*

This is not a performance exercise. It's a visual reminder that you were never walking alone.

2. Start a "Still Becoming" Journal

Each week, jot down:

- One moment you offered grace (to yourself or someone else)

- One moment you needed grace and didn't know how to ask for it

- One truth about God's grace you're learning to believe

Call it your *Still Becoming* journal, because healing isn't linear, and wholeness isn't about being done. It's about staying tender along the way.

3. Adopt a Breath Prayer for the Gray Days

Use this as a grounding rhythm when life feels heavy or unclear:

- **Inhale:** "Grace is enough…"

- **Exhale:** "…even here."

Repeat slowly, with your hand over your heart. Let it settle deep into your nervous system. Let it be your anchor when your mind spirals or your hope flickers.

4. Practice the "One Graceful Thing" Rule

Each day, ask yourself: *What's one graceful thing I can do today?*
It might be:

- Apologizing to someone (or to yourself) with softness.

- Saying no without guilt.

- Texting someone you love just to say "I see you."

- Letting yourself rest before you're exhausted.

- Choosing compassion over critique in a hard moment.

Small acts of grace ripple out. They change atmospheres, one quiet gesture at a time.

5. Bless Your Past Self. Daily.

Before you fall asleep each night, whisper this out loud:

"I forgive you for what you didn't know. I honor how you survived. I bless you for trying. Grace covered you then. Grace covers you now."

This isn't woo-woo. It's spiritual alignment. It's inviting the mercy of God into the cracks you once tried to patch alone. It's telling your old selves: *You didn't ruin the story. You made it here. And that's a miracle.*

Reflection Questions

1. **When you look back at your life, where can you now recognize grace, even in moments that once felt painful or unclear?**

2. **What parts of your story still feel too messy or unresolved to see through the lens of grace? Are you willing to let grace meet you there, even without answers?**

3. **What relationships, habits, or beliefs have been transformed by grace over time? How have you changed as a result?**

4. **How can you practice grace toward yourself this week, especially in your thoughts, your rest, and your expectations?**

5. **What does it mean to you to live a life "transformed by grace"? What small step can you take today to live that truth more fully?**

Closing Blessing: For the One Who's Still Becoming

May you look at your life and no longer see failure, but formation. May the broken pieces start to shimmer, not because they're perfect, but because they've been kissed by grace.

May you learn to trust the process, even when you can't predict the path. And when the road grows dark or the waiting feels endless, may you remember that grace is the hand holding yours, not the finish line.

You are not behind. You are not too late. You are not too much. You are not too broken.

You are becoming. And grace is making you new, again and again. So walk gently. Live honestly. And let grace have the final word. Amen.

www.ingramcontent.com/pod-product-compliance
Lightning Source LLC
Chambersburg PA
CBHW072348090426
42741CB00012B/2968